IT HAD TO BE
The Navajo Code Talkers Remember World War II

Stephen Mack

Members of the Navajo Code Talkers Association. Front row, left to right: Alfred Peaches, Kee Etsicitty, Jack Jones, Chester Nez, Alfred Newman; back row, left to right: Albert Smith, Samuel Tso, Keith Little, Wilford Buck, Samuel Smith, Bill Toledo, Jimmy Begay. Photograph taken in front of Trader Barb's Gallery, Old Town, Albuquerque on September 15, 2007.
Photo by Stephen Mack

Designed and published by
Whispering Dove Design, LLC

First published March 2008

Published in Marana, Arizona

Printed in the United States of America

Library of Congress Control Number: 2008925429

It Had to Be Done:
The Navajo Code Talkers Remember World War II

ISBN: 978-0-9728896-1-2

Whispering Dove Design, LLC
P. O. Box 1680
Cortaro, AZ 85652-1680

This book is printed on acid-free paper.

Cover design by Courtney Mack
Photos (front cover): *Iwo Jima Monument, Washington, D.C.*
Photo by Stephen Mack
Code Talkers, Albuquerque, New Mexico
Photo by Stephen Mack
Landing on Bougainville
Photo courtesy National Archives
Photo (back cover): *Monument Valley*
Photo by Courtney Mack
NTCA logo used courtesy Navajo Code Talkers Association

Dedicated to *Diné*

Acknowledgments

First and foremost, I wish to extend my deepest thanks to all the Navajo Code Talkers who generously shared their stories: Keith Little, president of the Navajo Code Talkers Association, and Samuel Tso, vice-president; and (in alphabetical order): Kee Etsicitty, Jack Jones, Alfred Newman, Chester Nez, Alfred Peaches, and Bill Toledo. Thanks also to Albert Smith, former president, who gave his blessing to this project. Keith Little in particular gave a considerable amount of time and attention to this project, for which I am deeply grateful.

This book would not have been possible without the help of Victoria Jarvison, who conceived the idea of the project and facilitated many of the interviews, as well as translated from Navajo to English for parts of this book. Thank you, Vicki.

Others whose contributions were essential for the production of this book include Sharon Culley, Archives Specialist, NWCS - Stills, at the National Archives in College Park, Maryland; Eunice Kahn, Archivist, Navajo Nation Museum, Window Rock, Arizona; Roseann Willink, professor of Navajo Language studies at the University of New Mexico; and the Pima County Public Library Infoline and Askalibrarian staff.

Gregory Cajete, Native American Studies Director at the University of New Mexico, and Lloyd L. Lee, visiting assistant professor of Native American Studies at UNM, have provided helpful feedback of the manuscript of this book, as have Debra Cordero, Stephen W. Stone, Rhonda Holdren and Leslie Rowe. Thanks also to Jeff A. Cherino for his help in some of the interviews, and Joan Gentry for her work in searching for images.

Profound thanks to my father, Courtney Mack, whose support made this book possible.

Table of Contents

INTRODUCTION

"If the Japanese had won … I wonder what would have happened?" Samuel Tso mused one summer afternoon in a Gallup, New Mexico hotel lobby. Mr. Tso, one of the surviving Navajo Code Talkers, was recalling a time over 60 years earlier when the question of a possible Japanese victory was not some frivolous intellectual exercise to while away a lazy afternoon. Rather, it was a looming possibility, and the outcome was far from certain. At stake was the very existence of the United States of America. World War II was a struggle of epic proportions, one in which the Navajo Code Talkers played a crucial role.

A threat to one's way of life was not a new experience for the Navajos. Back when the Navajo Code Talkers were children, there still lived some elders that could remember back to a tragic chapter of American history. Back in the year 1864, Navajos were forced—at gunpoint—to march from their homelands to a desolate location in eastern New Mexico in the dead of winter. Hundreds died on the enforced journey. Pregnant women were shot by American soldiers. Children disappeared. The Navajos spent four years in what amounted to a concentration camp before being allowed to return to their homeland. Stories from what became known as the "Long Walk" (or *Hwéeldi*) were passed down orally, often at social gatherings. Keith Little, another Navajo Code Talker, recalls: "The only way any of us remember is that the elderly people (the people that were born there, or were there and returned) … tell their tale about what happened." Others were very young and "barely remember coming back, or don't remember at all. But they woke up here. And their parents were captive, so that is the way they know." Mr. Little continues: "During the tales that they tell at some gatherings about some person, they will bring the certain person out: 'She went to *Hwéeldi* and came back,' or she was born there, or that person was born there."

Some of these survivors of *Hewéeldi* lived to see another painful event in Navajo history: the federally enforced livestock reduction of the mid 1930s, a time Keith Little himself recalls. "We lived through these forced reductions, forced regulations." He continues:

> They were forced to reduce their livestock. A lot of the horses were killed—just drove them into a corner someplace, and these policemen or whoever they were took a gun and shot each one of them. The same way with goats. There were too many goats. Goats were claimed to have eat up all the roots of the plants, or they chew on the branches and stuff like that. So they were the ones to go next. And then the next one was horses. Too many horses. And then the next one of course was the sheep. Sheep almost paid for everything that they have. It brings in income and give you meat. Sheep is almost used for everything. It pays for the existence of the people.

The effect, both on the economy and the culture of the Navajos, was devastating.

During the time of these forced reductions, on the other side of the world, events were unfolding in Asia that would have global ramifications, and the shock waves would ripple even through the remote Navajo Reservation, disrupting lives and changing the Navajo peoples forever.

Japan, operating under the policy of *hakko ichiu* (the eight corners of the world under one roof), began a course of conquest. In 1931, Manchuria, China fell to the Kwantung Army, an extreme nationalistic group within the Japanese military. On the morning of January 29, 1932, the Chapai quarter of Shanghai was incinerated by Japanese carrier bombers, killing thousands of women and children. That same year, Japan withdrew from the League of Nations. In late 1937, in an invasion involving acts of unspeakable cruelty, Nanking fell to the Japanese. Nineteen thirty-eight: Chiang Kai-Shek's government was pushed back to Chungking. Canton fell. Hankow fell. In 1940, Japan signed the Tripartite Pact with Germany and Italy, and the United States stopped exporting iron and steel to Japan. The following year, Japan invaded Indochina. In retalliation, the Americans, Dutch, and British imposed embargoes on steel and oil. The flow of oil into Japan was reduced to a trickle. Without oil, the Japanese Army and Navy would grind to a halt. But to obtain oil, Japan realized that war with America was virtually inevitable. It was decided to strike the U.S. first, without warning. On December 7, 1941, the Japanese attacked Pearl Harbor. Hours after the attack, Japan officially declared war against America. President Franklin D. Roosevelt declared war on Japan on December 8. Germany and Italy declared war against America three days later. The gauntlet was thrown, and the United States could no longer merely stand by and watch the atrocities unfolding in Europe and Asia.

During the few weeks remaining in 1941, the Japanese pushed onward. Guam was overtaken on December 10, Burma was invaded on the 11th, and Wake Island was captured on December 22. Hong Kong surrendered on Christmas Day.

The United States plunged into the war with a decimated fleet. Nineteen forty-two began with further Japanese victories, including the capture of the Philippines. The turning point for the Allies finally came on June 4, when Japan lost the Battle of Midway, the first defeat the Japanese Navy suffered in its history. From that point to the end of the war, the Japanese were on the defensive. The Allies advanced, wresting control—island by island—from Japan's grip. Guadalcanal was recaptured later in 1942, then Bougainville. The bloody battles on these Pacific islands dragged on over the next several years, culminating with the ferociously defended Iwo Jima and the invasion of Okinawa. And the Navajo Code Talkers, from Guadalcanal through the occupation of Japan, were there every step of the way.

Winning the war was a colossal achievement involving movements of men and artillery in numbers unprecedented in humanity's experience. These massive movements had to be coordinated, or else chaos would quickly ensue. To achieve this, codes designed to convey information with upmost security were formed.

The task the Marine Corps gave to these young Navajos fresh out of boot camp was to create a code that the best cryptanalytic minds in Japan would be unable to break. The 29 Navajo Marines (later known as the "First 29") entrusted with this task succeeded, finishing their job in seven weeks. Still, there were rigorous tests to be met. According to Simon Singh, the United States Naval codebreakers were challenged to break the newly-formed Navajo Code. (This is the same outfit that cracked Japan's Code Purple.) But after three weeks of intensive scrutiny, the Naval codebreakers were unable to crack the Code (*The Code Book: The Evolution of Secrecy from Mary, Queen of Scots to Quantum Cryptography* [New York: Doubleday, 1999], p. 196).

Nevertheless, there was a certain amount of skepticism, especially after several tests of the Navajo Code caused widespread panic among military personnel. The unfamiliar Navajo language was mistaken for Japanese, and it was thought that the Japanese were breaking into American radio frequencies. These incidents, along with a certain degree of skepticism born from prejudice, prevented the Navajo Code from being immediately put to use. It took time, but the phenomenal speed and accuracy of the Code gradually won over field commanders. The number of Code Talkers grew from 29 to a total of about 420 by the end of the war.

One Code Talker talks about their accomplishment as if they were just doing their job: another Code Talker refers to it as an act above and beyond the call of duty. Just doing their job? Definitely. Above and beyond the call of duty? Indisputably. Their duty as communication specialists was to pass information to the superiors, convey orders to the subordinates, and coordinate supporting efforts. And in this, they performed their jobs admirably. In battle, the task of the Navajo Code Talker was to: (1) receive a message in English; (2) translate the English words into Navajo *code* (not everyday Navajo)—in other words, they had to perform on-the-spot encryption; (3) relay the message via their radio to another Navajo Code Talker, who; (4) decrypted the message and wrote it out in English, quickly, accurately, and neatly. Often this was done under intense enemy fire. For this hazardous and intellectually demanding job, the Code Talker had to be fluent in both English and Navajo, as well as know the Navajo Code inside-out.

Keith Little recalls that "Code Talkers of a unit was always somewhere in the first or second wave of the landing force, the initial landing force. They lugged their radios in. They went as far inland as possible. They set up their equipment, many times under murderous fire by the enemy." Being communication specialists, they were often specially targeted by the enemy. It did not help that the old TBX radio had to be cranked (a very noisy process) to generate sufficient power for transmissions. Navajo Code Talker Kee Etsicitty remembers the older type of radio:

> There's no modern equipment. Radio was the old type, TBX they called it. It's a big old thing, gotta put that thing up … this was the kind we had. I guess over here in the stateside they were working on the new ones. Well, the new ones … they don't come to the Code Talker. They come to the ship first, or the headquarters first. They go over there first. The modern equipment—we don't get that. We still got the old type.

Keith Little was one of the fortunate ones who used the newer battery powered radios in the field. But he trained on the old TBX radio and recalls:

> You had a big generator, and the guy had to sit down on a stool and crank that generator. It makes a lot of noise. The cable around the front [connects] the generator to the radio set, where another guy is manning it. So there's two pieces of equipment; it takes about three people to lug it around. But in combat, I had a compact all to myself, portable compact. You don't have to crank it.

The Navajo Code is reproduced in Appendix 1 on page 72. A glance at the Code will reveal its complex nature. Often a code word was not a simple translation of words. For instance, there is no word in the Navajo language for "mortar," so the Code employs a description of a mortar, hence, `be-al-doh-cid-da-hi,` or "sitting gun." Sometimes, two or more Navajo words were used as a code for one English word, but the actual code word being conveyed involved the translation of the Navajo words into their English equivalents, and then the *fusion* of the English words into one. Navajo Code Talker Kee Etsicitty gives an example:

> Navajo language is something by description. If I say "hill" in Navajo, that means what I'm saying is "a lump on the earth." And "hill" is just one word in English, H-I-L-L. OK. Then when you send a message about the hill, you say "horse," and you put an "H" down. That's it. Then you think of "sick," you know, S-I-C-K. There's another word for sick: that's "ill." You know: I-L-L. So you see how easy that is? You take that "H" and "sick." "Horse sick" is what you say. You put "H" down and put "I-L-L." You put that together, that's "hill." So that's code word.

"Notice" in Navajo Code is `ne-da-tazi-thin,` which literally translates to "<u>no</u> <u>turkey ice</u>," hence, notice. These examples make it quite apparent why even one fluent in the Navajo language would not be able to understand a message transmitted in Navajo Code, and why the Navajo Code was never broken.

Readers will note the constant reference to the Code Talkers as "chief." On this subject, Keith Little was asked if being called chief bothered him. "No," he replied, "for me it didn't. It's just a common term, just like calling a friend 'Joe,' or something. It was always just like friends talking to each other. One calls his buddy 'chief,' and the other calls his buddy, 'Hey paleface,' or something like that, you know."

The following eight chapters consist of stories told to Stephen Mack (often with the participation of Victoria Jarvison) by the Navajo Code Talkers, stories presented in their own words. However, occasionally, small alterations were made. For instance, the tense of a word was sometimes changed to agree with the rest of the sentence. Repetitions of a word, which often happens when one is searching for the right word to use, were usually cut out. These alterations were made in the interest of clarity. Fidelity to their stories does not necessarily mean every filler word, every "you know," should be included. But even these words are often kept in the narrative. Just as errors in genetic transcription confers on every person their physical individuality, mannerisms in speech conveys an individuality of expression.

For the remainder of this book, the words of the Navajo Code Talkers themselves will be written in Times font, the same font you are reading now. The words of others, including interviewers and family members of the Code Talkers, will be italicized. Navajo words will also be italicized, for example: *anaalí*. For the words used in the Navajo Code itself, Prestige Elite font will be used: `wol-la-chee.` This differentiation is made because the spelling of the Navajo words in the Navajo Code dictionary (the spelling was made up by the First 29) is unique and differs from the current Navajo orthography—or all previous orthographies, for that matter.

Growing up on the reservation, Growing up at school

They punish you; kneeling down in the corner. Thirty minutes. And then they ask, "OK Sam, are you going to talk Navajo again?" And you answer with yes or no—in Navajo! —Samuel Tso

Keith Little in the early 1930s.
Photo courtesy Keith Little.

Keith Little, president of the Navajo Code Talkers Association at the time of this writing, discusses the background of the Navajo Code Talkers:

They [the Navajo] wanted to live their own way of life. And the reason behind the whole thing is that, in the beginning, they emerged right here, around the area someplace. That's according to the creation story. So that's where people came from. Their clans were created, their language was given to them, their prayers and everything—their religious belief, it was given to them. So ... their spiritual belief and the customs that the people observed is tied to the land, mother earth. And then the sky or the sun is the father; gives the natural things that people need to survive. So they're very well tied to the land. In other words, what is usually said is you get along with mother nature. You have to believe in mother nature, that your prayer—all your religious belief is tied to that. This is where they come from. The spiritual belief was tied to the land. So this is where the Navajo Code Talkers come from, this kind of teaching.

Not any of them was ever born in a hospital where they got a birth certificate, a record of their birth. There's none. Many of them were probably born in a hogan, maybe under a tree. Maybe even out in the open where the lady was herding sheep and went into labor, and give birth herself.

Aah, what I'm saying is most of the Navajo Code Talkers either were ... some of them might have been a little bit older than, older than the enlistment age; some of them were probably—most of them were probably too young. 'Cause they could not prove their age. *Keith Little himself signed up the day after his 17th birthday. But, he admits:* the birthday I have is just somebody's guess.

Keith Little in the early 1930s.
Photo courtesy Keith Little.

Chester Nez, one of the First 29:

Life on the reservation growing up was something that I have greatly enjoyed. My dad and my grandmother and my grandfather and my aunt were four people that kept an eye on me growing up. And I spent most of my time, those days and months and years, herding sheep. They had close to 1000 head of sheep. We traveled with the sheep. We didn't stay in one place. We moved. In those days we can move anywhere with the sheep. Nobody said this is my property, this is my land, you're not supposed to be here. Nobody said anything like that.

When I was old enough, about 10, 11, 12 years old, that's when they ... in those days the older people—the grandpa, grandma—they're the ones that told you what you are, your clan, and who's your relative, and all that stuff. It's all forgotten. The new generation—it's not there anymore.

Bill Toledo:

I lost my parents when I was a baby. My mother was injured, you know, during the springtime. And then my dad was injured from a bucking horse. So they, they were, maybe two weeks apart, I guess—they passed away from injuries. So I was raised by one of my youngest aunts, and my grandparents. They brought me up. Back in those days, we have sheep, horses, goats … that was our income, you know. When I was growing up, my grandparents were—especially grandma—was very strict with her discipline. You had to get up early, you know, even when you were small. Even when you're small you have to do your chores—go out in the corral and look after the sheep. And then grandpa would go jogging at dawn, so I had to go with him. I would just go a little way, you know, because we're small. You just go a little ways. And then as we grow up, we go a little further, further. Pretty soon we would outrun him, leave him behind. But he was good, you know, he was really … he never gets rough with us. Always teaching about life, you know, taking sweat baths when we were small. Grandma was on the other … it was different. She was very strict—was very strict with her discipline, you know. You gotta do whatever she says, and if you don't, you better watch out! She was just like … the eye. Really strict, you know. Really chews you out. As long as your follow her, you know—discipline, teaching—she was nice, a nice lady.

Vintage 1939 postcard of a typical hogan on the Navajo Reservation.
Private collection.

Alfred Peaches:

I took care of the sheep, cattle. By the time I was seven years old, I could ride on horseback. I could really ride—ride around. We had a flock of sheep, somewhere around about 700 to 800 head. Pretty close to 1000. It was hard work I did. I herd the sheep, take care of the cattle in the summertime. In wintertime we don't have to take care of the cow and the horses, they … they're loose out on the field. But the sheep, I have to take care of.

When I was about seven years old, my younger brother was put to school. He was the only student in the family. He had to go to about 75 miles away.

To where?

Tuba City, 75 miles away from my home. So he, while he was going to school, I had to take care of the livestock and all that. I wanted to go to school. I asked my parents. I wanted to go to school, too.

Jack Jones:

I was born and raised in the down the southern part of the state of Utah, southeastern part of Utah. And I been raised among the area where there were a group of Navajos and we are known as *K'aayellii* people. We consider ourselves (my people over) there as an independent group. And by that I mean we are not … we don't come under the main government of the Navajo Nation like it is in Arizona and New Mexico.

Samuel Tso, Vice President of the Navajo Code Talkers Association, recalls the epiphanal moment when he decided to go to school:

One spring, about the middle of June, I had been herding sheep all morning, And sheep and goats usually get thirsty at noontime, so I bring them back to the spring. This spring was up at a little higher elevation. All these red rocks … somehow the red stone keeps the water above it. It doesn't drain through. It stays above the red stone wall. And then the spring water seeps out between those there. And then the horses and cattle sort of have to climb up a steep to drink and go back up. At noontime I brought the sheep in to water. It was so hot! I didn't even have a hat or … I just let the sheep go drink by the spring.

And I just sit under the shade where some of the boulders are, under the shade. In a little while I heard a vehicle came in down below. I peeked out behind the rocks; saw a van stopped there. My cousins and my sister came out of that van and brought out their suitcases. They came up to the spring. They drank. They still don't know that I was behind the rocks. I just peeked out over there and look at them. Boy! Their hair was nice and combed. They had clean clothes on. They have shoes, nice and polished. After they drank they went on out to their suitcases. I didn't bother to greet them or anything. But after they went up I went over to the spring—looked at myself. Oh man. Saw myself in that pool of water. All that sweat, hair bushy, sweat tracks down the side of my face. When I saw their shoes I took a look at my feet. No shoes. All I noticed was that my feet were sort of caked with mud. My pants were was all torn up to my knee; just tied with a string. Took a look at my shirt; it was made out of a flour sack, stitched together. That's when I decided to go to school. I was either eight or nine. But even then I had to go herd sheep, because what little sheep we have, we were told: our lives depends on that sheep. It's in your hand to take care of it. I found out that's the responsibility I have in taking care of the sheep. Without shoes, go out there in a blazing sun.

But I think that day I remembered what my uncle told me. I don't know how old I was—either four or five years old. My father and my mother put me on a wagon. We rode wagons for some distance. When we got there, all I saw was a shaded—sort of like a wickiup, all joined together with no door except for a cloth where the entrance is. My father and mother told me, "Your uncle wants to see you. You go in there and meet him." So I get off, walk inside that wickiup. And he was sitting there, cross legged with a blanket covering his body there, just like the way they draw Indians—sitting there with a blanket. And then he motioned to me: sit down. So I sat down. And then he told me, "I wanted to see you and talk with you." Up to now, "Why me alone? There are my brothers and my sisters. Why me?" Anyway, he told me, "I want you to go to school." He says, "when you go to school, learn all you can, because you're going to need it," he says. "Me, I wished and wish I would have gone to school. But you, I would love for you to go to school." And after that, he said, "Me, I don't think I'll live very long any more. I have some kind of a disease," he says. By that time he opened his blanket, and he got sores all over him. I believe there was a lump here somewhere—some broken. And he says, "It really hurts," he says. With that, he closed his blanket. All he did was—he just hugged me, and then he sent me back out to the wagon. And I found out my uncle died that same night, by dawn.

Alfred Newman remembers:

I was raised in Coolidge [New Mexico]. My summer job was to take care of the livestock for the family ... do other work like hauling water, hauling wood—helping out the family that way. And the first time I started school was in Coolidge. And this school was a one room school where mostly Hispanic children were going to school. My folks worked at the Trading Post for the trader. My father did silversmith work, my mother did the weaving work.

So that one May morning a wagon came up to the trading post and there was Joe Silversmith and Dorothy Silversmith. We got in the wagon. There was myself and my sister. The four of us went from there on a wagon all the way to Rehoboth, Rehoboth Mission. We left about ten o'clock in the morning from the trading post, and we got to Rehoboth about five o'clock that afternoon. We stayed there overnight, and the next morning I was taken down to the school office where they registered me. And about noontime the folks had to leave, they had to go back. You know it's a long trip back to Coolidge, especially on wagon and horse. So they left us there.

I went to school there. I never saw ... well, I saw my folks about once every six months or something like that. Stayed in school all year. At the end of the school year we went to the highway, stopped the bus and went home on the bus, you know, Greyhound Bus. Stayed there, went to school there up to 1942.

Samuel Tso:

One day my cousins and my sisters, they got them ready, and they got the wagons ready to take them back to school. Me, I had to take the sheep out. While I took the sheep out, I saw them get in the wagon and move out. While I was over there to the side herding sheep, I decided: this is the day I'm going to go. So that's one thing a person that herds the sheep *never* does: to leave the sheep and go somewhere. But I did! I tried to follow the wagon. I couldn't catch up with it. But I guess my mother and my father, every now and then they check on me ... they probably saw me following the wagon. So my father saddled up the horse, came followed that wagon. Boy that wagon went along and I couldn't catch up with it. So he finally caught up with me. All he said was "get up in the back." So I just got up on the back and we went on. There was no word exchanged between us, my father and me. But halfway to school he finally said, "So you really want to go to school." And that was it.

When we got to where the school is, there's a Catholic church, a big Catholic church. We stopped there, and my father and me we went over to greet the priest. I never saw a house, I never saw a building, I never saw any Anglos at all, at that time. But this guy came out; he's got that hood covers his head, and a robe with something like a rope tied around its waist, and it has a wide sleeve. And he came out with his hands, both hands, inside the white robe and the hood pulled down. He has beard that cover all over him. I think he mumbled something about greetings in the Navajo language. When he took his hand out I saw his hand. His hand's white. But his face is covered with all that beard. Then after his hood he had a white forehead. So that's what we call *bilagáana*. *Bila* means "hands," *gáana* means "white." So in English that's Anglos. And then he fed us and we stayed there overnight.

In the morning we get up. He fed us again. And my father said, "Let's go to where there are many windows." Many windows? I never heard of windows at the time. He says, "*tsé soí łani*." *Tsé soí* means "rocks that you see through." *Łani* means "many." So I wonder what it is. So we went over there and there it was—this big building with windows all over along the side there. We went inside. And after we went inside there's a lady that came out, that greeted us. They took all the information about us. And after the registration, the next thing they do is, "You're gonna take a bath," they say. And you pulled out a basket, opened it; took a look at me. "I think this is your size." Government issued shoes. I look at it. Oh boy, that's going to be my first shoes. And then after I got that shoes, my dad says, "Take off the moccasin." He says, "That was your grandmothers moccasin that you were wearing to herd sheep." So I took that off and then the matron took me into what I found out was the shower room. And she gave me soap to go in there and says, "Wash in there. Wash all over your body. Take all your clothes off. Here, you put this on. Your socks, your underwear, your pants, and your shirt. After you wash, you put that on." So I went in there and I looked around. All I saw was water on the floor. So I turned around and asked the lady, "Where's the water?" "Oh," so she came over. "This is how you get the water. You turn this knob on. This one is cold water. This one is hot water. Be careful. You have to turn it on careful." So she helped me adjust it here. The water was coming out from there. Boy that really amazed me! Says, "You get underneath it. Wash your hair, all over. Here's the soap." I found out the soap is kind of slippery. I started playing with it. After I finished taking a shower and rinsed the soap off, and they give me towel. I reached for the towel and I looked out from the stall and I saw somebody way over there. Came out and look. So I just went back in and finished drying myself and then put on my underclothes. Then I found out I put on the underclothes the wrong way. She came in and started giggling. "Don't you have any underwears to wear?" I didn't know how to respond because I never had any. "So this is how you do it." So she helped me put it on. Then after I put it on, she left, pick up some of the stuff and took it. So I start following her, look out, and here somebody came out. And I start walking. And that guy start walking this way. And then what I discovered was, there's a big mirror standing there! When I came to it, I found out I could touch it, and I discovered myself. That was me. "Hey, that's me standing there!" I felt around and even my own face there. Afterward we went out and she showed me where my bed would be—mattress, sheet and blanket. "This is where you're going to stay and sleep." Boy, that was something! That's better than sheepskin. That's how I started school.

Jack Jones:

However, as time went on, when I was at a young age, well, I was sent to school in Shiprock. I must have been about maybe six or seven years old. They gave us the clothing that were military ... sort of like this color [points to a khaki green place mat].

Kind of light green or dark green. And they gave us to wear … they were all sizes, small, and they had sort of a slim bottom down there. And they gave us shoes, they gave us little pants, they gave us those coat, the same color, and we were all in uniform. And they led us to drill, to drill in formation. So we drilled, and at the same time I never knew any Anglo English word in any, like you say "no" or "yes," I never knew *nothing* as far as English, English language is concerned.

So that's the way it went, and … maybe one year, two years, three years, well, I begin to pick up some English words.

Alfred Peaches

So finally when I got to 15 years old, my father says, "OK, son, you can go to school. I think we can manage the ranch by ourselves." That's what they told me. So I got to school. I was a wild man, you know. I had long hair … regular traditional hair style. And I got to school the next fall, and therefore that was nineteen … 1939, I believe. All this time my brother had been to school, he never told me anything about "yes" or "no," you know, in English. So I didn't know yes or no—nothing. When I got to school it was kind of rough on me.

Alfred Peaches at school.
Photo courtesy Alfred Peaches.

At boarding schools across the Navajo Reservation, students were expected to speak only in English. The punishment for speaking just one word of Navajo was often severe. Bill Toledo was asked if he was ever punished for speaking Navajo:

Oh, yeah! Yes! Boarding school. During the school, when they catch you speaking … I think the government was trying to change your culture, to civilize you. That's what they were trying to do. When they catch you talking Navajo, they punish you. Then … I don't know if you ever taste those yellow soap. That's what they wash your mouth out with it, you know. And then sometimes in the livingroom, on those hard floor, they make you stand, you know, down on your knees in the corner for so many hours without moving around. But, after you wash your mouth out and clean your mouth out with soap and rinse it out and everything, you still go back and talk in Navajo again! [laugh] As long as they're not around, you know—jabber, jabber, jabber.

Samuel Tso was another with a streak of defiance:

They don't want us to talk our own language. When we do talk our own language, in secrecy, always somebody tells on us. And they come and says, "You've been talking Navajo." They punish you; kneeling down in the corner. Thirty minutes. And then they ask, "OK, Sam, are you going to talk Navajo again?" And then you answer with yes or no—in Navajo! [laughs] And then right there you get punished again!

Alfred Newman:

So there was a little kid, when I first went to school, when I first started school—he didn't know too much English. I don't remember what I said to him. This lady that took care of the dormitories, she heard me. And, boy, she comes running out. "Did you say something in Navajo?" I know she heard me, and I couldn't say, couldn't tell …. "Yes I did. I was telling him to make him understand." "Well, you know you're not supposed to talk Navajo under any circumstances," she said to me. "We'll have to correct that," she said. So she went somewhere—I don't know, it's where she keeps stuff; she tore a piece of that paper. "Sit down at that table and write 'I must not talk Navajo' 500 times," she said. So I started with a single pencil. When she wasn't around, I got two.

[Newman's wife, Betsy]: It was very strict, that school was very strict. To this day, people complain who went to school there how strict it was, and all that. But I don't know. We never, we never felt that it was very strict because we always, I guess you felt the same as I did, we always felt that it was for our own good, that we … for us to learn. Didn't take it as a punishment.

I didn't … I had no grudge against what happened at Rehoboth government school. At Rehoboth, we were told we need to learn English.

Chester Nez:

Oh, it was awful, man. I didn't talk or nothing. I kept to myself. I didn't want to ask question, I didn't want to answer questions and stuff like that. I almost came to—just a ball-like, you know. I didn't want to … matter of fact, I almost didn't have anything to do with that school. I didn't want to go to school. And I didn't know a word of English when I went to school. Nothing. It was mostly Navajo. So we stayed at this Tohatchi for almost a year. And my brother was the one that took us out to Fort Defiance, Arizona. That's where I begin to pick up "yes" and "no," "I want this," and this and this and that, and tried to learn the words in English, you know. It was very difficult in those days. Some of these people that worked with the Navajos, took care of us, they were *mean, mean* men. I always remember that and how they used to take a ruler, and put your hands out like this, and BANG THUMP THUMP THUMP, on the side. It was awful. I'll never forget that. Some of these people that mistreated all these young kids, small kids. That was real bad. I often think about those things.

How long did you stay in school?

Nine months. Nine months at school. Nine months. At the end of nine months that's when the kids took off. And there was another thing. When the school was out, some of these young kids—their family, parents would come and pick them up, take them home. But me, I was really too far from home. This one guy had an old Model T pickup, and he used to come and load us up and then take us to a place called Manuelito. It's on 66. He used to drop us off there. And I lived … from Manuelito to my place, was about 35 or close to 40 miles. He used to dump us off. We used to walk from there. Somebody, the older person that's with us, would take us home. We used to spend the night out in the open. When the sun goes down, we build a fire and we spend the night there. The next day we started walking again.

How old were you?

I was about 10 years old. It used to take us about two days to get home from this Trading Post, walking. In those days it was very difficult. It was so hard. Transportation. There was no cars, no nothing. Mostly walking.

It was real bad, man. Those people that work for the government, some of our own peoples, how they used to treat us in those days. Man, it was real bad then. They'd kick you and they'd hit you, slap you, knock you down. It was awful, growing up in government schools. I was thinking that it was something I'll never forget, the way they used to mistreat us. I used to feel sorry for some of those little boys, five or six years old—they get kicked around, crying. Bad. But later on it got a little better. It got a little better later on.

Alfred Peaches:

I remember one guy was teaching us. He was a German. When the war started, they took him away. Other German people were being watched, I guess. So was the Chinese, Chinese and Japanese, especially Japanese. They round up all the Japanese; they were camped down here, Leupp. They were holding Japanese down there. It was a big camp, campground.

Samuel Tso:

In June, we're finished high school—don't know where to go. I thought the federal government would provide transportation for me to take me home. All they told me was, "There's a road down that way to the main highway. Either turn right or turn left. There are towns there, there are jobs available." So the only thing I could do is pack my suitcase, start walking down the road without any money. No money. Walking down the road about a mile down the highway; that suitcase was real heavy. All I could do is look … bailing wire or some kind of rope. But I found some old rusty bailing wire. I looped them around, hooked it on the suitcase and put it over my arm and shoulder. And I pad it with a jacket that I had, and I start walking again. I get real tired. I sit down. A car passing by; they won't pick me up. I went down to the main highway and this suitcase was in my way, so I decided to hide it across the road somewhere. That suitcase was in my way.

The shortest way was to Gallup, the longest way was to Grants and Albuquerque. So I decided to go to Gallup. Left my suitcase there in an arroyo. (It's still there. I never went back to pick it up. It's still there.) I finally probably walked halfway to Gallup before someone picked me up and dropped me off in Gallup.

Tired and hungry. No money. That night I just went out of the main town, I went up on top of the hill, and I just found a rock, so I sat on top my jacket, and I went to sleep there.

In the morning I got up, went back down to the bus depot, and I just washed my face, and asked for jobs here and there. No jobs. Just before noon I was getting desperate. Where could I get some money? I went over to the railroad station. Usually a lot of Navajos get hired on the railroads as common labor. I went over there and … I told them I was only 19. And they don't employ 19 year olds; you have to be 21 years old to work, so I just left. Before I went out the door the guy said, the guy that interview me said, "Why don't you come back this afternoon? We may have something for you."

So I just hung around that building until one o'clock. I went through that building door again. As soon as I walked through that door, the man that interviewed me said, "Did you say you're 21?" Boy that really stunned me! All I could say: "Yeah, yeah, yeah! I'm 21!"

"So we put you on a train this afternoon and go on down to California, put you to work there."

"How am I going to get in there?"

Says, "You don't need to worry about it. On this train, when we hire you, we'll put your name on our list and you can eat on borrowed money from your work."

But, I'm still hungry. I just walked around and found a ... one Navajo man used to go to school at Fort Wingate, and I found out he's working. I asked him to loan me five bucks. "When I get paid I'll double the money to you." He finally did. He loaned me $5.00. And then I know a place where ... they call a place "Lucky Lunch." A Japanese owns that cafe. You can eat there—a hamburger for 25 cents, five cents a cup of coffee. I went over there and I ate over there. And then with what I have left, I'll have lunch when I go to work.

Sunday December 7, 1941

Something that's beyond our comprehension
—Keith Little

The bombing of Pearl Harbor. The USS West Virginia, with the USS Tennessee in the background.
Photo courtesy National Archives.

Bill Toledo recalls:

When I was 17 years old, I was going to school in Crownpoint, New Mexico. And December 7, 1941, when the Japanese attacked Pearl Harbor, I was 17 years old. And we had a little tiny radio, and the news came on: the Japanese attacked. So all these kids, we all bunched up, listening to the news, you know, and we're asking where Pearl Harbor is.

Alfred Newman:

Me, I thought, well, Japan, that's a little island. Of course I heard about Japanese taking over China and all that, conquering those big countries. And I thought, well … the United States would take care of them in a few months or a year or something like that, I thought. Some of the other guys said the same thing. That's what I thought when—well, it'll be over before I get out of school.

And here you had to go over there.

Um-hm. That was wishful thinking.

Alfred Newman was attending school in Rehoboth, New Mexico, along with his future wife, Betsy. She recalls that day also:

Some of the students cried, I guess. They were scared. It was frightening news, especially they kept doing it over and over, you know. And, uh, some of the … some of the girls, some of the students cried. They were scared.

Keith Little:

Well, I distinctly remember that. I was in a boarding school, mission boarding school in Ganado, Arizona. They call it Ganado Mission School. It was Sunday. The food was always bad—institutional food—and it was never enough. So we supplement the school food with what we can get on our own. Like on Sunday afternoon, after noon lunch, we know we're going to get sandwiches in the evening: dry peanut butter sandwich, maybe with a boiled egg, dry and kept for a long time. Not fresh. And then maybe jam. Never a meat sandwich. It's always peanut butter or jam, and maybe with a boiled egg; and sometimes an orange or an apple. This was our Sunday meal, evening.

So what we do, some of us do, somehow we get a hold of coffee because we learned to drink coffee at home. It was the dominant drink with the meal. No milk. And if you don't have it then you use water. So coffee and tea were the dominating drinks.

So at this mission school we did what we can to secure some additional food, in addition to what we get on Sunday evening. And I'm going to say that one day we were hunting around in the trash pile. Somebody had thrown away a .22 rifle. It didn't have a firing pin, but somebody else had gone into Gallup and gotten a firing pin. We tried it and it worked. Single shot. So we cleaned that rifle up real good and we treasured it because we can go hunting in the evening or Sunday. Kill a few rabbits, clean them off, dress them up, hang them up, air them out; then we build a fire with lots of charcoal, and then we roasted it over the charcoal. So this is what we were doing.

And we brought our sandwich in the dormitory, and we all sat down to eat. And somebody say, "Hey, you guys got some salt?" No, we look at each other and found out there was no salt to season our meat. Goddang, we gotta have salt! Our best runner in the group was sent back to the dormitory to steal some salt from somewhere.

So he came back—he was all panting, he had really run hard. He came back. We looked at him and said, "What's wrong with you Joe?" He was panting and wheezing, trying to get his breath. He said, "You know what? The United States's been bombed." He said it like that, "The United States's been bombed."

We looked at him, astonished. What did he say? "What did you say, Joe?"

"The United States's been bombed."

"Where?"

And then he said, "Something called Pearl Harbor." Where is Pearl Harbor? Where is Pearl Harbor, anyway? I guess one in the crowd had studied a little bit about Hawaii. He says, "I think Pearl Harbor is in Hawaii. I think. I'm not sure," he says.

"But that's not United States. Hawaii is way away in the middle of the Pacific Ocean someplace. That's not United States."

"Well, it belongs to the United States. They say it's a territory of the United States." So the radio says United States's been bombed. So instead of—he brought the salt back all right, but we just gathered our sandwiches up.

We listened to the radio in the dormitories—see what he said. So we went back to the dormitory and listened to the radio. Everybody was quiet really. Usually the living room is really a noisy place to be, but this time everybody was trying to listen to what was going on, what was being said on the radio. But it was in the Hawaiian Islands and the United States Naval Base at Pearl Harbor had been bombed at eight o'clock this morning. Here it was five, six o'clock in the evening. So the thing that I heard was President Franklin Roosevelt was talking on the radio. He says, "This is a day of infamy" he says. And I distinctly remember that. Because I didn't know … what is "infamy"? So they condemned the Japanese naval forces for sneaking on a United States Naval base in Pearl Harbor. Our matron, the house mother, was standing there with us listening. And she—every time something drastic is said over the radio, she said O-o-O-ooh! [Keith Little chuckles softly when recalling the house mother's reaction] That's how come I remember all these things. "But tomorrow the Congress will come to Washington, D.C., and they may have to declare war." O-o-O-ooh! she says.

"Why are you so worried, Mrs. Simon?" somebody said.

"Because a lot of the young men are going to get killed for nothing," she said. And we were not even thinking about that. Something kind of foreign.

Recruiting & Training

Everything is shining on him; shoes shining, all the brass on him shining. Dress blues. And we all wanted to be like him.

— Bill Toledo

The First 29 prepare to leave for the Marine Corps Depot in San Diego, California, May 4, 1942.

Group on left side, left to right: unidentified, John Manuelito, unidentified, Charles Yazzie, Cozy Brown, Chester Nez, David Curley, USN Officer, Sam Begay, Carl N. Gorman, USMC Officer, unidentified, Eugene Crawford, USMC Officer, Major Frank Shannon.

Group on right side, left to right: Dale June. Frank Pete, Wilsie Bitsie, James Dixon, Benjamin Cleveland, Lloyd Oliver, unidentified, unidentified, Oscar Ilthma.

Photographed by Milton Snow. Courtesy of the Navajo Nation Museum, Window Rock, AZ. Catalog #N07-121.

The use of American Indian languages as a form of secure communication goes back to the First World War, when Choctaws were used to relay messages in their own language in the battlefields of France. The enemy was taken by surprise, and the experiment was considered a success.

In 1940, another experiment was carried out by the Army Signal Corps in Louisiana, this time with the Comanches. The idea was abandoned because of the lack of equivalents in the Comanche language for words such as "tank" or "submarine." The Comanches and Choctaws substituted words in their language to describe military terms, a practice that was perceived as a weakness. The irony of course is that it was precisely this substitution that gave strength to their codes as well as the Navajo Code. It created what has often been described as a "code within the code," so that even one fluent in the Navajo language would not be able to understand an intercepted message.

Chester Nez:

Back in 1942, around about May, these recruiters came to Tuba City. They were looking for some young guys to join the Marine Corps. So there's a roommate by the name of Roy Begay, and I told him, "Why don't we try out?" So he says, "Let's go." So we went up to this guy, and we told him that we'd like to try to see how we was going to make out. They registered us — I think there was five of us sitting on stools. And then they took us to Window Rock, and there must have been about 200 or close to 300 young men — some of them are older, overage. And all day, they try to get these guys to remember when they were born, how they grew up, what their job was, things like that. And I just waited around all day that first day, and they only took — I think it was 26 or 27. We spent the night, and the next day they tried it out again, see if they can maybe two or three more. So the next day they got 29, and the recruiters got ready, and they told us we're about ready to move out of Fort Defiance. So they moved us to Fort Wingate. And there, we waited around for maybe two or three hours. And in the evening they took us to supper with the students, and when we finished our supper, they took us back out. And there was a bus there. We boarded the bus there. It must have been about 6:30 or 7:00 in the evening. And then we took off, said we'll be on our way to San Diego.

So we left Fort Wingate and we traveled all night. And it must have been about close to five or six o'clock in the morning when we got to San Diego. This was on Sunday when we arrived in San Diego, so we couldn't do nothing. We just took it easy all day. And Monday they gave us uniforms, took a medical examination, and all that stuff. And all the 29 went through. No problem. And so we started … they told us all kinds of different stories, then they showed us a movie about Wake Island. It was a story about how the enemy came in, the Japanese, and how they fought them and everything like that. And then we started our training. It took us seven weeks to finish boot camp.

The idea of a code utilizing American Indian languages may have been dropped by the Army, but the Marines revisited the idea in early 1942. Bill Toledo:

It came from a white man that grew up learning the language. It was his idea. He sent it to the Marine Corps …

The First 29 are sworn into the United States Marine Corps at Fort Wingate, NM, by Major Frank Shannon. May 4, 1942. Photo courtesy of the Navajo Nation Museum—Milton Snow Coll. #NO7-53.

Do you remember his name?

Philip Johnston. Yeah, he talks [Navajo]; you can understand him, you know. He don't talk real fluently, but you could understand him. He grew up among the Navajos in Leupp, Arizona. Then he served in World War One where he found out that the army was using the Oklahoma Indians, you know, using their language in the war.

Chester Nez:

I guess Philip Johnston talks to the commanding general and now they tried them out, from what I understand they tried to make up a code. And there was some Navajos that were working in Los Angeles. So they got these guys—three or four of them—and took them to San Diego, and they tried them out. They wrote out a message; and they had one section here and another section over there of Navajos. They wrote out a message and they sent it to one another. And it worked out perfect, perfect. So they decided … Johnston was the one that really puts himself to develop a code in our own language. And that's what we did.

Chester Nez:

And after we finished boot camp they took us on to a place called Camp Elliott. Camp Pendleton wasn't built at that time. There was no Camp Pendleton. It was Camp Elliott. So we started to make up a code.

One morning after breakfast this major took us into a big room like this. And he told us that we was going to make up a code from A to Z in our own native language. And we were kind of surprised to hear something like that. We didn't know what the hell he was talking about. He left the room and locked the door behind him.

They started out talking about how we was going to make up that code from A, from letter A we started different kinds of animals, the names of animals. The alphabet starts with an A so we decided to use the red ant, `wol-la-chee`, so that was A; and then B was a bear; C was a cat, C; D was a deer; E was an elk, and all down the line. It was very interesting. We finished the code. We talked about it and went back through the whole thing again and tried to decide what we was going to use. We had changed the name of, or leave it just the way it is. So we finally came to the conclusion that we was going to use what we made up as the code. So we started training and training and training for about 13 weeks, and tried to develop and memorize this code that we made up at Camp Elliott. I think it was in November when we were ready to ship out. And we all got together—decided how we was going to be divided up. At that time they only had 1st Marine Division and 2nd Marine Division. The third was just about to start to form a division, so I went with the 1st Marine Division, and then the second divide us up into two groups, and we shipped out that November 1942.

Twenty-seven of the First 29 were shipped off to the South Pacific; the other two remained behind for recruitment and training purposes. One recruiter visited the high school in Crownpoint. Bill Toledo recalls the visit, and the events that followed:

So I went back to school, and about the last part of October 1942 a young Marine came to our school, you know, a Navajo Marine. He was all dressed up in blues, his dress blues, you know, and real sharp. His name was Johnny Manuelito, and he must have been about maybe 19 or 20 years old. 'Course at that time we didn't know that he was a Code Talker. He was already trained, you know. So he wanted to talk to all us 18-year-olds, and so we all assembled in the auditorium. And he talked to us for about maybe 45 minutes. He talked about all the good stuff in Marine Corps, the good life: you get to travel the country, the world; and all about the liberties we would have, the weekends and all that. One thing he never mentioned was boot camp! And of course we were really, you know, we were really listening, because he really dressed up real nice, you know, and real sharp. Everything is shining on him, you know; shoes shining, all the brass on him was shining, you know. Dress blues. And we all wanted to be like him.

So after he got through, five of us got together—three of us from the Torreon. And one ... was Frank Toledo—you always see his picture, you know, those two guys, Preston [Toledo] (you always see him in the books or on TV, you know, sitting there by the radio); and myself, and then two other guys from Crownpoint, Ralph and Herbert Morgan. So five of us got together and we talked it over, you know. So we decided to join. We were all 18 years old so we don't need the parents

PFC Preston Toledo (left) and PFC Frank Toledo.
Photo courtesy National Archives.

permission, you know. So, so we all decided to volunteer.

And they sent us to Fort Wingate to have our physical. We all passed our physical, except Preston. He, he was about maybe two or three pounds light. So he start, he start complaining, you know, that he don't want to go back to school. He wanted to go with us. Said, "Think of something!" he said, "I wanted to go with you guys!" he said. So the recruiter said, "after you guys have your lunch at the school, come back and we'll recheck you." So we start teasing Preston, you know, that he should put some rocks or sand in his pocket. "Don't make fun of me!" he said, "I'm serious!" he said. So after we ate lunch, you know, Frank came up with a good one. He said, "Why don't you go back over there to the kitchen or to the washroom and drink, drink a lot of water," he said, "as much as you can stand." So he went back over there; and we went back to the recruiter and he weigh us again, you know, all over again. And Preston passed. He must have gained maybe about five or six pounds. He was happy. And he went with us. He was with the 1st Marine Division. He died last year, in November [2004]. Accident, you know, around between Crownpoint and Cuba. He ran into a horse at night. And Frank Toledo, he died in 1970. And then the other two guys, Ralph Morgan, he was killed in action in over there by New Guinea. And I don't know what happened to Herbert. He's … his cousin, I never knew what happened to him. So there was five of us that, you know, we joined.

Alfred Newman remembers the day his stepfather brought a letter home:

Let's see … I was about 17, 18 years old. And, uh, then one day my stepfather brought the letter back. I opened it and read it, and it was from the U. S. government, asking me if I was interested in joining the Marine Corps. It said we have a special assignment. If you are interested report to Fort Wingate school. So I said, "Well, I guess I'll join the Marine Corps and see what it does." I didn't think they would accept me because I wasn't a big husky macho man: I was a little skinny Navajo boy. So I hitchhiked down there. My folks didn't have a car or anything, so I hitchhiked to Wingate.

I don't know how many guys were there. We were all put in … we all went into a building, and there was a Marine Corps sergeant there, and he had a Navajo interpreter with him. And he asked questions, or he told us the Marine Corps wanted Navajo men … he didn't say what he wanted them for. He said we just like to have some Navajo Indians in the Corps. And so we all signed our name, and told us when to report back. And he said you'll be taken to Santa Fe for your physical. There you'll be accepted into the Corps if you pass the tests, physical tests. So about two weeks later, we got on

Standing: Recruiters Cpl. John Benally and Johnny Manuelito.
Seated: Rex T. Kontz (bottom step); the remainder are unidentified. Fort Wingate Boarding School, October 5, 1942.
Photographed by Milton Snow. Courtesy of the Navajo Nation Museum, Window Rock, AZ. Catalog #NO7-38.

the train in Gallup, went to Santa Fe, and went through our physical. There's a whole bunch of Navajo boys there. I mean there's all size and shape, and those that were accepted into the Marine Corps went one way; some went to the army; some went to the Navy. So I was told to go into this other line, and so did Joe Silversmith. We went at the same time there.

Alfred Peaches:

It was time to go back to school, so I came back to the reservation; registered at the school, and they put me in 6th grade class. I was only in 6th grade then. And I was in the class for about a week and then I went home one day, one weekend, And when I got home my mother says, "Son, go to trading post at Kayenta. Get my mail, get any mail I got down there. Bring it back to me." So I saddled the horse and took off, 20 miles away, and took off early in the morning—got there about noon. He took my mother's mail. And there was only one mine: it was a draft card. So I brought back the mail and some groceries, back to the house, and I told my mother. I read the draft card. It says report at a certain date—I forgot what the date was—anyway it says ... I told her, I told my mother I got a card from draft board. I had to go to. They told me to go down there, go to examination, go to service. So that I told my mother. And she says, "OK, son, whatever they say, you go down there."

Keith Little enlisted in March 1943, the day after his birthday:

I got permission to ride the mail bus from Ganado Mission to Gallup. That evening I had to stay in a motel, and then go to a recruiting station, a Marine Corps recruiting station because a lot of my friends had joined the Marine Corps, and I wanted to be one of them. And somewhere—I think it was at the post office somewhere—that I had seen a sign saying that the United States Marine Corps are the greatest fighting men in the world. So that was a drawing power for me.

Mr. Little was sent by bus all the way to Phoenix, only to be told to return to school to finish the year.

But when they sent me back, they gave me a piece of paper and they said "You carry this with you when you get back to Ganado. Get somebody—your guardian, somebody that takes care of you, to sign it so you can enter the Marine Corps."

So I went back to Ganado and in the meantime a fellow that I got acquainted with, a Navajo boy—same age as me, I guess—we went together to Phoenix and came back together, and we talked about—we didn't talk about our age but in the process of talking, he brings out the fact that, "You're 17 years old?"

"Yeah, I'm 17."

"You gotta get your guardian to sign these papers." He says, "You know what? If I go to my father, he's going to say no. He's not going to sign it, my mother is not going to sign it, my grandpa is not going to sign it. Tell me to herd sheep." So he says, "I know a man out there, I call him *anaalí* ... so we'll go talk to him."

So the next day we got out of the confinements of the boarding school where we stayed, and went walking over to this guy's place. He was taking his sheep out when we got there. And we asked him—well the guy asked him, he says, "You want to thumbprint a paper for us?" (He asked him in Navajo.) And the guy, without even asking no question, he says, "Sure, bring the paper." So we brought out the paper, and then he says, "Where's the thumb printer?"

No thumbprint pad!

"Well," he says, "you don't have it. You want me to thumbprint a paper for you?"

"Yes."

"Well, go find a thumb printer someplace. I don't know where; go steal one if you have to," he says. So we walk all the way back to the boarding school. All the conversation is in Navajo. Look around different places, offices. Every one of these office people, they ask us what we want. We asked a certain question. We knew we would get a negative answer. So about noon time, close to noon time, the superintendent of the agency, I guess it was him (somebody in the high official because he had an old suit on), he left the office and left his door open. And right on the desk there was a little black box; and my friend runs over there and picks it up and look at it and stuck it in his pocket. "Let's go."

You walk all the way back up here: Fort Defiance, the junction—way back in there, he was herding sheep, way in the corner in the rocks. We found him up there. And he laid the paper out on a flat rock; told him to put his thumb right here. That's what he did, he put his thumb right there. On my paper, he puts his thumbs on. Now we're OK, and then we started to walk on. "Hey, come here, come here! What did I do that for, anyway? What is that?"

"We're going to where they're fighting. We're going way over there to California where we're going to learn to fight. And then we're going to go overseas to fight the Japanese."

"Good, good, good," he says. We started to walk on. "Hey boys, I'm going to tell you something," he says. He puts his hands on our shoulders. "Now you guys, when you get to where they're fighting, I want you to kill just as many Japanese as possible. Now get going," he says. So that's the way we got to the Marine Corps.

Samuel Tso's liberal manipulation of his age caught up with him one day at work. He remembers:

I went to work over in California. Not even a month later the draft board came around while we were working on the railroad, checking our registration card for service. When they came around, I told them, "I'm 19."

Says, "No you can't be 19. You can't work on this railroad when you're 19. You've got to be 21."

"So, OK, I'm 21."

He says, "You go over to the draft board and register there." So I have to take the day off that day and go to San Bernardino, California; register. Not very long after that Uncle Sam called me.

IN THE SERVICE

Alfred Newman was a part of the 297th All-Navajo Platoon. He recalls his first days in the Marines:

I don't remember how long it took us to get to San Diego on the train. You know, it used to stop at all these little places, like Barstow, Flagstaff, and all along to

California. I think we got there late in the … or some evening, either the next day or something like that, you know, the evening. And just … just herded off to a tent area where there was nothing but what they call "tent city." We're just all … all in line. The sergeant—the drill sergeant—met us there. There was three of them. They all put us in lines and said now you're in the Marine Corps, and you do this and that. They march us over to the tent area and they just said OK, you five, here; you five, there; you five, there—went down the line, put us in the tent. There were cots in there with a mattress on it. For the first night they say, "Here's a blanket," and he just threw a blanket at us, and we went to sleep that way.

The sergeant said, "Tomorrow morning you'll hear the reveille. I give you 15 minutes to shower, shave and shampoo," he said. So we all, we all went to bed when the … well the taps was already blown, I guess. We just went to bed. And the next morning, I figured … well, I couldn't sleep. It's all new to me and I've never been away from home, that far away, and everything was strange to me. The only place was that school. Of course it's right within an area where my folks could see me, you know, but this was miles and miles away. So I was kind of a little leery about everything.

When the reveille blew, everybody was rushing over there, trying to be first. They had a long building with showers and wash basins and commodes on one wall.

From then on I got onto routine. That day, we went through the medical part. We had to strip down and we marched by the doctors and we marched back around this way. And there's some men nurses with syringe on each side—we walked down there, poked us here and poked us here. And on down the line, we went to the quartermaster, same ol' same building, quartermaster's section. They threw us the uniforms, say, "here." They just look at us, just picked out what they call fatigues or dungarees; they just threw it at us, on the table: all the underclothes, the dungarees, top, and a hat to wear. We marched a little further, we stepped on a scale, they weighed us and at the same time they look at the measurement on the scale on our, for our feet, for new pair of shoes. I told him, "This shoes is a little too small." He says, "Well, what do you want to do? Go barefooted? Take it or leave it." So that was it.

Back to the barracks when we all got done; the sergeant was waiting there. We all got dressed up in our new uniforms, and, "Fall out," and blew the whistle—"fall out." So we all went out there on the parade ground, fell in formation, and had a roll call. He had trouble pronouncing some names, Navajo names. One guy, his name was Etsicitty. He just called him "Electricity." There's some other names he had trouble with, but he got them straightened out. But that Etsicitty got him every time!

So that was our first day. Our first day there, we started marching. We were just all stumbling around, and trying to keep in step. And the poor little guys that were small, put the taller guys up front, and couldn't keep up with the taller boys. They had to skip around to try to get in step. Drill sergeant got a little disgusted. Well, the first day wasn't so bad; I guess he had a little patience. The end of the first week I guess he had enough. He started cussing, calling names and, "Hey, you stump jumpers,* let's get in step!" Boy, I mean, he used foul language. He'd go up to you, look you in the face, just tell you off, what he thought of you. And he told me, "Sonny boy, you better put that razor to work!" he says. "Shave that peach fuzz off!" he said. I didn't think I

*stump jumper: World War II-vintage slang meaning a Marine from a rural background.
(Paul Dickson. *War Slang: America's Fighting Words and Phrases from the Civil War to the Gulf War* [New York: Pocket Books, 1994] p. 219)

needed to shave then, so … but he told me that, so the very next morning I did.

And that was the routine every morning: drill, breakfast, reveille, go do what you had to do to clean up, and the whistle would blow and you fall out in line, drill a few times; then I guess they had a schedule, how you went into the mess hall. While we're waiting we did calisthenics or drill. You know, you go to the mess hall, fall in line, single line, pick up a tray—pick up a tray, and a cup, knife, fork, and spoon; walk along the table where they had all the food. The Marines serving, they just get a great big spoon, they just fwawped it in your tray. You can't say I don't want it. If you say I don't want it, they said "You better eat it!" I ate everything that was given me. And some guys, you know, after they got a little acquainted, they says, "I don't want that!" Says, "You better eat it, Marine!" he say, And then they go along.

After you finish, you go by this garbage can. Now all the stuff that you don't finish, like bones or peelings or something, you scrape it out of your tray. If you leave some fruit in there, he says, "All right Marine, get over there and finish eating that!" pull you off to the side and you have to eat it. That's the way it was. You don't have nothing to say. You can't even look at the sergeant cross-eyed or what do you want to call it. He'll tell you right off. "You dumb [—]," he'll call you.

Bill Toledo:
And after we got our physical, they sent us down to Phoenix where we officially joined the Marines, you know, and from there they sent us down to boot camp. And then we got to the Marine Corps base, you know, and we start lining up for haircuts. And then always in the Marines they call you Chief, you know. And you get up to the barbers, they say, "Chief, how do you want your hair cut? You want a light trim or a close cut?" I say, "I just want mine trimmed real nice so I look nice." Well, your hair went off, cut, they just zoom zoom zoom, you know. Your hair's about that big! And everybody got a real short hair cut.

And then after we got our clothes, you know, Marine clothes, dungarees, and we're in a new uniform, you know, and you start, start learning how to march, you know, and learning, learning the command and all that, you know. And it was, it was kind of funny. You know, those GI's were really strict in those days, you know. They don't hold back on anything. If you make a mistake, they really cuss you out. Really rough with you. And they gave you a command: half of us would go that way, the other half go this way. Another command: we would bump into each other; and us guys, you know, we thought it was funny. We really laughed about it, and then we would get chewed out. After about a week or so, we straightened out. Everything just goes real nice, you know, marching, command at the same time. It was really nice, you know. We did a lot of running, a lot of exercise.

One thing I had a habit of doing was when we get in a formation, I always had my hands in my pocket. We were told about it, you know. Keep your hand out of your pocket. If you're out in the combat area and the enemies catch you with your hand in your pocket, you're a dead Marine! So one morning the DI caught me with my hands in my pocket. He came over and … (I don't know if you've ever seen that movie about Gomer Pyle and the DI? He always comes up to Gomer Pyle face to face and chews him out.) That's what he did, you know, he came up and chewed. I was looking down his throat, all going like this, and standing at attention: "Yes sir! Yes sir! Yes sir!" And he was chewing me out about my hands in my pocket. Said, "Go back to the tent area," he said. "Get thread and needle." The beach is just a little way from the Marine Corps base. "You run down there and put wet sand in your pocket." We had a big pocket in these dungarees, you know. "Fill it up and sew it closed." Went down there and put sand in my pockets, sew it closed. He said, "Be sure and mark it where you took the sand out." I was carrying that sand for about two days. After two days, he told me to go back to that area where I took the sand out. You know those tides, they come up and fill it back up. I couldn't find it, but I had a marker, you know, so I put it back in there. I learned my lesson.

Jack Jones's experience in the military-styled school in Shiprock paid off in Boot Camp:

So then I … the drill instructor, he teach you how to march. Well, I thought to myself, I know all of that. I know how to march. So it was no problem for me to learn to march, you know, all the different marches, the command, and all. I knew it all. So from there, this sergeant asked me, he said, "What kind of Indian are you? What tribe of Indian are you?" I said I'm a Navajo. He says, "You know, there's a group of Navajos over here, a whole bunch of them, platoon." And he says, "Maybe I'll send you over there." And so the arrangement was made; they took me over there. I met a bunch of Navajos over there, a whole bunch of them. And they were to learn the Code Talk.

Samuel Tso:

So I went through basic training in Marine Corps base in San Diego. One whole month and then two weeks. Then we're sent out for advanced training. We had a practice shooting. They didn't have to teach me that because I already know how to hunt prairie dogs. I can kill a prairie dog about 50 yards away, with their eyebrows just above the ground. I can shoot that. I made expert rifleman. They were talking about me, training me for sniper because I held the Marine Corps shooting record for a couple of months. There's another guy that came in from somewhere — from Ozarks, joined the Marines and broke my record.

Anyway, after that advanced training, we're all shipped out. Here, the guys that I trained with—the advanced training—they were shipped out. They took my sea bag and put it to the side. The rest of them went on. Me, they sent me to Camp Pendleton. I said, "Hey, my buddies are going there, so what's the matter with me?" They said, "You're going to a special service group. You're going to be training in a special service. It is said that you are really needed there." And then I found out that I have to go to a Code Talkers school. When I joined that Code Talkers school I found out they are forming a new division—a 5th Marine Division, they're being formed. And I was selected to go with the reconnaissance company. We train up in the mountains. We train out in the desert. We train out on the beach. We train out on the island. And we train out at sea.

Kee Etsicitty:

Then you gotta go to the rifle range, you gotta go this way, you gotta go do that training. A lot of training. Then, at the same time, they screen you again; and say hey, you talk a little bit of English. They got what they call Code Talking School. They're working on it. Uncle Sam wants you guys, Navajos.

Keith Little:

But anyway, when I enlisted I knew nothing about it. This was in 1943—May of 1943—I went through the recruit depot in San Diego. During the process of my training I was asked if I was a Navajo. I told them I was. "Are you a Navajo?" "Yes, I'm a Navajo." The only thing the instructor said was, "I understand that the Marine Corps needs Navajos badly because they're good scouts." So that's how I got into the Code Talkers school, simply because I was a Navajo.

Alfred Peaches:

Four weeks; get out of boot camp and you chose what outfit you want, like artillery unit, amphibious, radio. So I chose something, I don't know what. They said to me, "You have to go to Oceanside, California," he tells me. "You're going to be a radio operator," they told me.

Bill Toledo talks about learning the Code:

And they make about 211 codes that we had to learn. So this school building was … you had bars, you know, all on the windows and on the doors. All the entries had bars. They has security outside and inside, walking around, seeing everybody's doing their … this was one of the secret schools, you know. We were being watched all the time. They wouldn't let us carry notes on us while we were studying. Everything we had to learn, we had to memorize. All these, all those 211 words we had to memorize, all the way into the night. And then during the day we would be schooling, using the code out there, by telephone, message—use the message, how to use the coded message.

Was it difficult?

Yeah, it was hard at first, you know. Then after we caught on, it was kind of easy. The Marine general was the one that said that these codes, that these words have to be something that would become easy to remember. So that's how they made it. And, like "tank" was "turtle", and `chay-da-gahi` is a turtle.

Jack Jones:

So there we were. And so from there, well, it was not much time, you know, given to us to learn code talking. They give whole bunch of names like that, the names of the ships, the names of different kinds of weapons. And then there was alphabet—you got to learn how to spell this and that. And so sometime—lots of time on the message, well, you had to use that alphabet.

Frequent use was made of the alphabet, and so it was decided to have multiple words for almost every letter of the alphabet. (The complete Navajo Code, including the words for these letters, can be found in Appendix 1.) The reason for this is because repetition creates patterns, and cryptanalysts look for patterns which can provide the key to unraveling a code.

Kee Etsicitty:

We tell each other: don't never say anything about Code Talking, not even with the outfit that you're in; your best friend, don't tell him about this. You're with the communication people, you're in the Marine Corps, that's what you tell them. That's all.

Samuel Tso remembers a thwarted reunion:

After we passed all that tests, we found out that we can go home to see our parents. So they bought tickets for us and all that, and let us go. I went as far as Winslow. The bus doesn't come this way. From Winslow it goes down south. At Winslow, when we got off the bus, there was a military police came out, calling our names. They gave me a letter, and that letter said report right back. It says you have to get ready. The other guys got their letters, and I found out they just ignored and went on home. Me, I was told to come back right away, so I just went back. So I never saw my parents or sister again.

Bill Toledo ships out:

They don't tell you where you want to go, you know. So you just individually know where you're going to be assigned. So I was assigned to the 3rd Marine Division, 9th Marine regiment, headquarters 3rd battalion, communications the radio and telephone section. They took me over to Camp Pendleton that evening. The 3rd Marine Division were getting ready to move out overseas. So I joined this communication outfit that evening. And I was introduced to these guys, you know. And later on I found out that these guys were talking about me. They say that I was assigned to this communication as a Japanese interpreter. They were told not to talk to me or ask any questions, you know. But anyway, we all got acquainted anyway even though they told us not to talk to me, you know; I was still talking to them. And I got acquainted that evening. And that's when I joined these guys and I was with them for about three years.

The next day we moved out to San Diego, moved out to San Diego harbor, where we boarded one of those big troop ships called Mount Vernon. And after we boarded ship, you know, we set sailing. And one thing happens to you when you boarded ship and you've never been on it, is that you get seasick. And everybody was hanging over the rails. It took us about two weeks to get down to New Zealand. We got down there in February. It was winter over here when we left; it was summer down that way. And on the way to New Zealand we crossed the equator. So they told us to put on our winter uniform, you know, wool uniform, winter green. So we put it on and got on topside and stand in the sun for about one hours. This guy's falling over from heat. And I've been through these sweat lodge, you know, and I guess that's where it help me stay up when we were initiated, crossing the equator.

● ● ●

Alfred Newman:

Some of our Navajo boys got homesick, I guess, when those waves, when they rise like that. And you look way out there, and you think there were sheep coming. The sheep were coming home.

4

On the Battlefield

*They were shooting at us, and we were talking to
the 2nd Marine Division, sending messages back
and forth—that's all we did was send messages;
messages coming in and going out.*
—Chester Nez

On the island of Peleliu.
Photo courtesy National Archives.

The Battle of Midway took place while the Navajo Code was still in its formative stages. The first major battle employing the use of Navajo Code Talkers was Guadalcanal. Chester Nez recalls:

We sailed aboard ship for about a little over three weeks. We came to this island called New Caledonia. It's a small island. I guess the island belonged to the French people. And we stayed there about five—I think it was five months. We trained and memorized all this code that we made up and used it, you know, to transmit the message back and forth. We went on day and night maneuvers.

Alfred Newman:

We were like that for about two weeks, two weeks or more to get to New Caledonia. When we arrived there, the ship docked, and there we sit again, just waiting around, waiting around. Used to watch those hammerhead sharks swimming around the ship. And those seagulls would come around and boy, they bombarding you with their droppings!

After we stayed there about two weeks, and it rained all those two weeks, it rained and rained. Some of the guys were going nuts. What they were doing was sneaking off the base and going to these natives over there that were making some kind of brew that they make of their own. They call it Butterfly Juice, you know. That's what they guys called it. They drink that and they go nuts. One day we're standing in the chow line, and this guy just started yelling and jumping around, screaming and everything else.

Was it because he drank that Butterfly Juice?

Butterfly Juice and coconut; you make liquor out of coconut juice.

And that's why he started screaming and all that?

Yeah. Yeah, I guess it's just like dope or something, the way they make it, I guess.

Chester Nez:

So finally, I think it was on April or May, they told us that we was about ready to ship out to invade Guadalcanal. We boarded ship again and then we sailed for about almost two weeks. And we saw the island w-a-a-a-y up ahead: that was Guadalcanal. And it was really cloudy; and all the battleships and all the planes started to bombard this area for about maybe two or three hours.

And when we're ready to board the landing crafts, we got off the ship and got on the landing craft and circled about and hour and a half. And then we started out, hit the beach. And it was raining really hard, it was just raining, coming down. And then me and my buddy, all we did was dig a foxhole and stayed down in there. They told us not to move, just stay in your foxholes. They were bombarding us and we would shadow those people. It was real hard. I mean, they … our foxholes had water about that much [gestures]. We was sitting in the foxholes.

So the following morning—was told us to move on, so we fix our pack and then we started out. Started to walk, and you could see all the dead Japs, you know, laying around. It was something that I had experience, you know; it's awful to really try to understand what happened, and how everything was going to go, and who's going to be lucky or ….

They were shooting at us, and we were talking to the 2nd Marine Division, sending messages back and forth—that's all we did was send messages; messages coming in and going out. We'd received a message about supply and ammunition and food and medical, and then relay reports on who got killed and how many soldiers were lost and who needs different kinds of supplies. That's what we were talking, sending message back and forth. And at that time it changed, but we never had a chance to rest. I mean this was the first, second day that we were actually in the war with the Japanese. At first, you know, you're not too sure whether you're going to get hit or you're going to get killed, or something like that. It's very difficult situation. I tied to get myself to be cool, to get my mind set on what I'm doing—on the message that's coming in, and answering the particular message, and sending them off. It was very hard. That first, second, third day was awfully hard, really hard.

Guadalcanal, 1942.
Photo courtesy National Archives.

Bill Toledo on Guadalcanal:

We have air raid from other bases, you know. There's Japanese bases; those bombers, they come in. [The] Army, they have these anti-aircraft guns, you know, located different areas of the islands. And they had these searchlights, too, that'll go way up into the sky to spot these bombers when they come over. Then they shoot at it with these 90 millimeter anti-aircraft guns. And they come over and they drop bombs, you know, in different areas—mostly on the airfield, that airfield they call Henderson Field. And they got a lot of these Marine airplane there, call it Wildcat fighter plane. Sometimes, during the day, we watched these dogfights between the Marine fighter plane and the Japanese Zeroes. Every time a Japanese Zero gets shot down, everybody hollers, you know, clapping, and yelling. And some of those Zeroes, they get shot down. Then when we find those wreckage, you know, we get a

Bill Toledo
Photo courtesy Bill Toledo.

piece of those scraps, ornaments, scraps from the plank. And these Marines, they bring it over, and they used to bring it to me, and I'd put trees on there, you know, palm trees. "Just draw us something on there," you know. It's sort of a souvenir.

Bill Toledo recalls landing on Bougainville:

We landed there on Bougainville on November 1st, 1943. They didn't use me during the landing. My colonel commander was a very strict ... this guy never smiled, he was always serious, you know, he was always giving you straight command, and never smiled. And I don't know why he never used me in the landing. We had a bad landing that morning. We landed on the slopy area like this, so a lot of those landing craft got stuck on the beach. So we're trying to pull them back into the water, and there's a Japanese base on the other side of Bougainville. I guess they found out that we landed there, so the Japanese Zero fighter plane, they came over and they strafed that beach while we were all on there. And then our aircraft carrier was a little ways out in the water; guess they notified them so they sent them fighter planes, chased these guys away and shot them down. And we had a hard time in that landing.

The first waves of U.S. Marines approaches Empress Augusta Bay, Bougainville.
Photo courtesy National Archives.

At night, two guys, they share a foxhole. Communication section, you know, we move behind the front line, front line troops, you know. We furnish communication for the unit that we're in. So during the landing they never used the code. I guess the others, they used the code. So one night, about two nights later I think it was, a coded message came in for the radio man. And my partner, he carries a little machine: they call it Shackle cipher.* You feed the numbers and letters into this machine and line them up, you know, where you get the message out of it. So these guys, they tried to get the message. I don't know how the message was written, but anyway they were having a hard time with it. An hour went by. Two hours. Three hours. The commander was getting discouraged. And my partner was out there with the radio man, trying to get the message out there. And then finally the colonel said, "Get Toledo on there, and see what he can do." So my partner comes crawling back into my foxhole. I cover myself with a canvas, and flashlight. I call the Code Talkers at the regimental headquarters—John Kinsel. And I asked John, "What was in that message that you sent to us?" So they got it, sent it to me, and I got it in less than three minutes. And there it was: where we were going to go the next morning, you know, for the front line troops; one of the company was going to make a move, certain areas on the front line. It was the message that these guys were trying to get. From then on, I got the job for

*According to Lieutenant Commander Paul E. Ruud of the U.S. Navy, "Japanese forces broke the 'Shackle code' method of encrypting map coordinates during Operation Forager [Saipan] and also imitated valid operators." (*How Much for a Pound of Communication?* Marine Corps Command and Staff College document written in fulfillment of a requirement for the Marine Corps command and staff college. 1997.) This made the Navajo Code even more valuable because it was never broken, and Navajo radio operators absolutely could not be imitated.

the rest of the war because my code was faster. And the faster you send the code, the faster you receive, and save somebody's life.

Anyway, the commander was really impressed with that. Me and the radio man, my partner, we always follow him around wherever he goes, you know. If the front line troops want a round of ammunition or water or ration, he would write a message, and we send it in code back to the regiment headquarters.

Chester Nez was on Bougainville, also:

And then the commanding general told our outfit that we were going to hit another island. That was Bougainville. It's a lot bigger than Guadalcanal. So we boarded ship again and we started out sailing again for a couple of days. Then we hit Bougainville. The same thing, the same situation, everything was about the same as Guadalcanal. Just keep on fighting and fighting, day and night, day and night. And this took us about almost three months to secure that island again.

Alfred Newman:

We had to establish a perimeter for the for the army to take over … real thick jungle, great big ol' trees just covered everything. You could hardly see up through the trees. And all of a sudden we heard a plane, and pretty soon we hear CRACK CRACK CRACK CRACK, and shells bursting. It was 25 or 20 millimeter or something. And somebody yelled out, "Hit the deck!" and we all did. And somebody—I don't know, this communication officer was in the back somewhere. One of the guards said, "That's our own plane! That's our own plane!" I think it was a lieutenant that said, "Throw that smoke shell out there!" It's a yellow smoke shell; a grenade is what it was. They just pull the pin out and throw it way out there. It emits yellow smoke, it shows friendly troops from below. They just made one pass. They didn't come back, they just went on and I don't know where they went.

And then we got to where we were supposed to go. We bivouaced again. And then they told us, "This would be a permanent position here, so fix you foxholes good. Sandbag them." So they threw us empty sacks and we had to sandbag our foxhole. And we waited, we just waited for our next order, and we stayed there about a week.

Word finally came through: he says, "You better advance up the hill." I guess some of the army troops had already pulled back. So we went up, went up, went up there and, uh, I had to help carry parts of a machine gun. And every now and then we'll hear sporadic fire from up in front of us; I guess they were Japanese snipers or something. I don't know whether they were taken care of or not, but anyway, we just all hit the ground every now and then, and just keep going till we got to the side of the hill. And on top of the hill was … a lot of wounded guys up there. They said that they couldn't get them down. So he says, "We want volunteers to go up there." So they say, "You. You. You. Go up there." We carried stretchers up there, carrying our rifles and looked around there for wounded. There were some already dead. They were dead for about two days. Some were still alive. One guy had his head split open right here, and it was just full of maggots. And while the corpsmen were giving him first aid, we were waiting to carry him out on a stretcher. Henry and I were kind of close together. And all of a sudden we heard a Whoosh BOOM! It landed, oh, I would say about 20 feet from us. There was this corpsman—I think there were two of them—they were working on this soldier that was injured. He was still alive, and I think there were one or two still alive—the rest were all dead. And fortunately that thing hit the tree, the bomb. And, uh, I think two or three of them came down, but they were old shot. And this one corpsman that was working on that wounded man, he had a piece of shrapnel right on the center of his back, and he's working on that man; he just sat there and didn't say a word or nothing. He just fell over. Guess that shot got to him, and he … he was dead when he hit the ground. He was sitting there next to the soldier, treating him, giving him first aid.

And we only take two live guys off that hill; the rest were all dead. When everything quiet down, we all went down that trail with stretchers. The jeep ambulances were all waiting down there. We put them on there and went back to the rear echelon.

Kee Etsicitty recalls a more relaxed moment in Bougainville:

The planes come in. One day a bunch of them came in, Black Sheep—that's the name of the squadron that came in. When they come landing in, they had this Corsair plane, you know—the wing of them drops down like that and comes up like that. They call them Corsair, they call them. They come in there, a bunch of them—maybe, I don't know, about 18 of these guys. They were training in New Zealand. They come there, refuel at that place, go on to Rabaul, I think they call it. We talked to these guys. Some of them, they're friendly guys. Hey, what are you guys doing? These, there was one, two, three of them got this little red flag painted on their plane. And there's one fellow, kind of skinny like that. He had, I think he had 14 of those flags. I talked to him. His last name is … Boyington, the ace of World War II. He had shot down more Japanese planes than …. He said that the Good Lord would take care of them; you know, he talks like that. He talked to us. We told him we're Indians. We talked to that guy. Yeah, he says, you're doing all right. (He doesn't know we're Code Talkers. We didn't say when we talked to him. Everybody done their job.) Then they took off, going to Rabaul. Oh, about a couple of days later, he's the one that got shot down. He went to prison. I don't know what happened after that,* I never heard about that. But he was the ace, he was the one that … Marine Corps Ace, they call him.

Bill Toledo on Bougainville:

And then these Japanese, they were real good jungle warfare. They'd sneak through the front line, and that's what they'd look for: trails, you know, where we string wires. When they find one they keep it on; they carry a telephone, they keep it on there, and they listen. And when they hear us talking, then they try to discourage us. Sometimes when these guys are talking English—these other Marines, they hear these Japanese talking, they call us. And so I call John Kinsel, you know, start talking Navajo. "Did you get a letter from home? What's going on over there? Is there a squaw dance going on?" or something like that; just talking and joking and laughing. And then the Japanese, they cut the wires, you know. And then these telephone wires people, they had to go troubleshooting.

And that's how we used to discourage them: by talking to each others, you know, telling jokes and all that. And they would holler at us. I don't know what they were

*Major Gregory "Pappy" Boyington (1912-1988) was shot down January 3, 1944 and was held captive by the Japanese. He was released August 29, 1945.

saying, but anyway they cut the wires.

Chester Nez remembers more training and leaving for Guam:
    And then my outfit, the 1st Marine Division, moved back to Guadalcanal. We did some more training. After that training the 1st Marine Division, my outfit, was told that they was going to a rest area, and this rest area was ... I don't remember whether it was Australia or New Zealand. And the 1st Marine Division took off. There was ten of us Code Talkers that ... they left us at Guadalcanal. We didn't go with that division to take a rest period. So the 3rd Marine Division came in; that's where we had a chance to join the 3rd Marine Division. So we didn't go for a rest period. They kept us there on Guadalcanal; and we went out, did some more training, stuff like that, and landings and all that, you know. It was a lot of hard work, day and night.
    And after that, we were ready to travel to Guam. That's the third island, Guam. It took us about ... almost three weeks to travel aboard ship again. And the 2nd Marine Division was right with us that Division, 2nd and 3rd Marine Division. The 1st Marine Division went to Australia for a rest period. So the 2nd and the 3rd Marine Division, we were supposed to hit Guam, and the 2nd Marine Division was supposed to hit Saipan. So we divided: they went their way to this Saipan, we went on to Guam. It was the same old story, the same thing, we had to go through the same situation — taking shots, wounded and everything like that. We spent almost two months before we secured Guam. And then from Guam there was about 2- or 300 of us that went back to Guadalcanal for a rest period. And the commanding general traveled back from Guam to Guadalcanal, and we stayed there for another ... I think it was about three months, training training training training.

Bill Toledo remembers Guam:
    Anyway, after Bougainville was secured, we moved back to Guadalcanal. We had a rest day, about a week we rest up, then we started training again, training again all through the winter and spring. And July 21, 1944, we're ready for combat again. So we move up from Guadalcanal to Guam. Landed there on the 21st of July, 1944. We landed there in the morning. And communication captain gave me a flag. We had this landing craft that's ... they called it an amphibious landing craft, where it travels on water and land. It's like a tank; it floats. Anyway, we're all bunched up ... a whole section ... all bunched up ... they're all standing by the captain, they were standing right there. Here's that exhaust, in the middle, inside — big exhaust, real hot. They were pushing me against it, you know. All the shells dropping around us, you know, during the landing. The captain gave me a flag to plant on their beach when we land. So, I was more worried about being ... get burned, you know, from the exhaust, because these guys were all, we're all packed in there like sardines. And the captain, here he was all sweaty, you know. I guess he was shaking. He must have been scared. Finally we all climb up and drop off the landing craft and planted the flag on the beach. And then we move on. That's when our colonel got shot, that morning. And that captain never landed. I guess, I don't know, I guess they took him back to the ship, you know. He never landed. I guess he must have got scared or something. He was all shaky. Never saw him again. Anyway, we landed there and ... I saw that picture of that monument on the beach on Guam. These guys brought their pictures back at the meeting,

where there's a big monument there, where the 3rd Marine Division landed. Yeah. Well, Richard gave me a picture, too, of that area when he went back one year.

Alfred Newman had just made it ashore on Guam:

And there's Gustine and myself and one lieutenant—he was supposed to be the one that was supposed to give the locations of the area where the ship was supposed to fire. And we were supposed to transmit that back to the ship. He gave the coordinates of the area according to the map. And Gustine and I was supposed to send it to the ship, in Navajo. We were waiting, waiting. The early notice was the first wave wasn't so bad. The Japanese were all hiding, getting out of area where the shells and bombs were falling. It got kind of quiet for maybe about, oh, 15-20 minutes. That's when we went ashore.

No sooner the planes and the shelling stopped, here comes the Japanese fire. Machine guns and mortars and stuff like that. And we had to crawl around with the equipment. That lieutenant, all he has was a clipboard and I guess a few pencils in his pocket [laughs]. He just crawled around and stopped and looked for a place to get to, out of the shelling area. But in the meantime, these guys that were in the second or third wave, boy, they were just getting hit. You hear people screaming, calling for medics, corpsmen, people hollering for help. And we just kept going. And this lieutenant, he just all … was shocked or something. He was … he didn't know what to do. He said, "You Marines are crazy," he says, "running into all that firing." We didn't say anything. We know we had to get to a safe place without being shot or bombed or something like that. And we found a place, a little, a little hollow in the ground. That was a natural hollow, a dip in the ground, and there's a coconut tree growing kind of … an angle like that. And the lieutenant went over there and sat down against that coconut tree. We set up our radio and, uh, Gustine said, "I'll send a message." So, OK, I'll run the generator. And it was one of those things [TBX radio] that you just CRANK CRANK CRANK CRANK until you get enough power. I guess he didn't want to do that.

In the meantime the Japanese were throwing shells and mortars, and one of the mortars landed real close. I happened to be down in that little dip, ready to work the generator in case we got a message. Gustine was sitting up high, and the lieutenant was sitting down, leaning up against the coconut tree. He had his clipboard here—and a piece of shrapnel went through his hand. Right through, very clean; didn't hit his body, just his hand. He says, "I'm hit! I'm hit!" and he was really hanging onto his hand like this and he was bleeding. And told Tully, he says, "Get over here." So he went over there; he tore off his first aid kit and just put a compress on each side, and just wrapped it up for him real tight. He says, "Well, fellows, I guess I won't have to go," he says. "You can go back to your company," he says. "I'm no use here." We packed up our gear and we wandered back down over to the headquarters. And from then on, it was just moving up right behind the front line troops, being shot at and shelled.

Bill Toledo:

It took us about from 21st of July to August 10th [1944], when we secured the island. But a lot of those Japanese, you know, they took to the hills; some hiding in the jungle, in the caves. So the general told us that we're going to sweep the island again. So the division landed … landed across the island, you know, started moving north.

Got rid of a lot of those that were hiding. And then on the east side, that's where we camp, set up a camp there. We rest up for about a week, and then start training again. And we trained all through the summer, into the fall, into the winter. And February, we're ready to go again.

There has been controversy over the issue of bodyguards for the Navajo Code Talkers. Bill Toledo remembers a conversation that took place during a 1988 automobile trip to San Francisco with Richard Bonhan, an old war buddy:

On the way up, we were talking about what we did in the war, you know. And I had heard from the other Code Talkers, you know, when we have a meeting in Gallup, that some of them had a Code Talkers bodyguard. And that's when I mentioned that to him that I heard that some of these guys here had bodyguards, you know. "Yeah," he said, "and you had one, too!" he said to me. And I never knew, you know. I guess he did a really good job of it 'cause I never suspected that he was assigned to me. Everything looks natural. We worked together, you see, we were assigned to a foxhole together, and we spent the night in foxhole. And we worked together in communication—he used the radio and I used my code, so everything looks natural, you know. Sometimes I guess when he's not with me, they would assign somebody to me. Never suspected.

But I did get away from him, on Guam. One night … one night, we were … we were attacked at night by this Japanese, they call it banzai attack. A banzai is when … is a last resort in … Japanese, they run out of ammunition, they run out of everything. And they're …they got no … no hope. So they just attack you with whatever they can come up with at night, you know. And they'd be hollering and screaming, and all that. So that night they destroyed our radio and telephone. So that morning one of the sergeants gave me a message, said, "Toledo," he said, "take this message down to the regiment headquarters right away," he said. And then I wasn't supposed to be used as a runner, but I had to take orders, you know, 'cause he's a sergeant. I was only a PFC. So I guess Richard didn't know that he gave me this order, you know, so I took off. I was coming down behind the front line along the road. It rains a lot, too, on Guam. The mud was about that deep on the road. I came to this one truck. They're loading these dead Marines, you know. They were bringing them down off the hills in ... in wire ... wire baskets and ropes, they string them out. And then these guys, they get a hold of them; these guys—they're just like logs—get a hold of their legs, and then their other side. They just swing them over and they just put them in the truck. And these guys were all piled up in the truck, too, like logs, you know—these dead Marines.

There was, on the other side, there was a gap in the hill, and all these Marines were on the other side. And there was a gap through here, real muddy. So I started. And I didn't know there was a sniper down here, somewhere down in the canyon. Anybody was coming across would be get shot at. Nobody told me about it. So here I come with a message. I started walking, you know, and pretty soon I hear bullets zinging by. I took off and I fell into the mud, and I got out and took off again ... ahhh, real slippery, you know. I was all muddy. Bullets zinging by, you know; zig-zagging like the football players, you know, zig-zag like this, you know. And all these guys were hollering, "Get off the road!" So finally I got over to where the guys were, you know, and I got there without getting hit. Then one guy came up to me, he said, "Hey Chief," he said, "where did you play football?" [laughs] 'Cause he saw me zig-zagging like this. And that's when I found out there was a sniper out there. We look up there, and he was up there, started going up towards the top. There was a Marine up there at the top, laying down, you know. He came right up to him and he shot him there. And then everybody saw that, you know, so everybody started walking again. And then I went on down to the beach and delivered the message. And I came back up. And one of the ... John Kinsel is with the regimental air corps, down there. Guess one of those guys were up here where I was. I guess he knew me. So I guess he told John that, "Hey I saw your buddy up there," he told him, "I saw your buddy up there. He outrun the bullets over there," he told him. I guess when he was shooting the enemy, you know, came through without getting shot. When I saw John again later, he told me, "Hey, I heard you outrun the bullets. How did you do that?" John always tease me about that.

Anyway, later on when we're driving up to San Francisco, I was telling Richard that I delivered a message down to the beach that certain day on Guam. He said, "You delivered the message?" he said. "Who told you to do that?" And I told him the sergeant, his name was Bill ... Billy ... let's see, what was his name?

"You know, he wasn't supposed to do that," he said. "You're not supposed to deliver the message," he said.

"Well, I didn't know," I said, "nobody told me." So, well, anyway, he was kind of upset about it, but this was long after the war.

Chester Nez recalls a case of mistaken identity:
And that evening one guy came over and said, "You guys can secure gather all our equipment together and report over to that tank over there," he says. That tank was about 250 yards from where we were. So we got ready to start off. We started to walk off that place where we were. Some army guys came by and they took us for Japanese. I had a pistol, a .300 pistol to my head; and my buddies, those other guys, had a rifle on them. We didn't know what to do. We were kind of really scared. You know, these guys was going to shoot us. We told one of the guys, "Go over to that tank way up there, and get one of the lieutenants, or somebody, from over there to tell you

guys that we're with the communication outfit." So one of the army guys went over there and he got a lieutenant over there. He brought him back. And he told these guys, he said, "These are my men. They're working with us. They're a bunch of Marines." So these guys didn't know what to do, and the lieutenant told these guys, "I want to see you guys in the morning." I don't know what they do to those guys. [laughs]

Another case of mistaken identity involved Bill Toledo:

On Bougainville, I think it was the second day after we start moving on, off the beach into the jungle, and the front line troops were right in front of us. They were moving through the jungle. We were right behind them. And one of the riflemen, we're all mixed, they're were all mixed with the communication guys, you know, riflemen. And as I was going in, moving with communication there, one of the riflemen poked me with a rifle in the back, told me to raise my hands, and told me to turn around, you know. So the colonel was far away from where I was. So he took me over to the colonel and told the colonel that he just found this Japanese among the Marines, and he's wearing the Marine clothes, the Marine dog tag. He says he's a Marine. "What should I do with him?" he says. "Shall I go ahead and shoot him?" The colonel says, "let him go," he say, "he's one of our men." So when I look back over there, he was getting chewed out.

Right then and there, I guess my partner, foxhole partner, I guess he told my partner, he said, "He's your man." I guess he told him to see that this don't happen again. I guess that's when he realized how important we were, carrying all that code around, you know, and he don't want the general to get after him if he loses me. So he was assigned as a bodyguard, without me knowing it.

Kee Etsicitty:

So they took care of me; my officer did real good. They tell you to move there, move here, do this. Some of them, some of [the Code Talkers], they say they didn't have no bodyguard. Your officer's your bodyguard. They take care of you. That's what they told us. You can't go anywhere without letting the officer know. Nowhere.

A Code Talker's bodyguard potentially faced a grim prospect. Jack Jones:

They assigned each Code Talker a bodyguard. And the instructions to that battalion or company: if you see a Code Talker captured, shoot the Code Talker, 'cause he's got all the brainwork on the code, you know. So that was an order. But never a time, I never heard a Code Talker been captured.

The Code Talkers themselves faced a grim possibility. Kee Etsicitty:

One day when we were there, there was a guy that was—and I remember his name real good 'cause he's a colonel, full fleshed colonel, got a chicken on his shoulder—his name was Colonel Robinson. One day he come over to our tent where the Code Talkers were. He came in there and he had the holster, you know, and a pistol, .45, one of those heavy things, make you walk like that, you know. He said, "This is for you Code Talkers." That's what he told us. "You don't use this pistol on anybody. This is for *you*, when you get captured, that's when you cock that thing back, put it here [Etsicitty points to his temple], goodbye." And he went.

Alfred Newman:

And we had one Code Talker that got killed over there: Johnson Housewood was his name. And he was with his uncles, his two uncles. They were together. Guess they landed on the second or third wave, and that's when most of the firing goes on—when the firing from planes, and bombing from planes and ships cease. That's when the Japanese really go to work. And I guess for cover a bunch of them all jump in a great big bomb crater. And it just so happened that one of the mortar shells landed right amongst them and killed them. And he was one of them.

About, oh, three or four o'clock, word came up that he was killed on the, on the beach. I never saw those, those two other guys anymore. I guess they left or … I don't know what happened to them. I never saw them again. They were all together all the time. So after that, the Guam campaign, we never … well, I never saw them again; I don't think anybody saw them again.

Kee Etsicitty:

Over there on the old type of radio, the Japanese would get on your frequency, they come in—boy, they cuss you out. Boy, they talk English, they tell you to go to hell, anything, anything. You have to switch on them. On Guam when we were up there, this one guy by the name of Kinsel, Johnny Kinsel—he's the one that was talking, that was sending message. And the Japanese, one of them got on our frequency. He come up, say "I went to school at the University of California, Los Angeles," he says. "You know what? Franklin Delano Roosevelt eats shit," he said. And ol' Johnny Kinsel, he come up and say, "Yeah, Tojo eats shit, too!" and then he switches on.

Blasting a pillbox with TNT at Peleliu Island.
Photo courtesy National Archives.

Chester Nez moves on to Peleliu:

And then they told us that we were ready to go hit another island. We hit Guadalcanal, Bougainville, Guam and we was going after the fourth island: Peleliu. Peleliu Island. That's almost as big as Guadalcanal. Boarded ship again and took off again, sailed for about another two weeks, almost three weeks before we hit Peleliu. And there was an airport must have been about two and a half miles from the beach at the airport. The airport was here and we landed right almost at the center of the airport. Peleliu I think was the worst island that I took part to take it back. It was really hard. There more Japanese there than any of the other three islands that we hit.

Jack Jones remembers Peleliu Island:

The first night, early in the morning in the dark, just beginning to see, we heard a yell from that hillside all the way along the, coming out of the jungle there. We look up. There's a bunch of Japanese, they're running, you know. They had their gun toward us. We have to get our head up, get our rifle and start shooting them. I don't believe anybody got killed because we were all in a, in a dugout, foxhole. And the fire from that hillside still was so … rapid firing, you know, down below where we were. We couldn't run, so we stayed there on the second day.

After the second day, the commanding officer said we've got to have air support. (If some officer, they want a point of a hill to be hit by a big gun, they give him the number. Every hill had a number.) And so he ordered air support. And it quieted down after that, and we were ready to move out of there.

I stood up. You see, some of my comrades were all in there, they dug in. A few bombs hit, and one of them hit pretty close where I was. All I heard was a, was a noise, and I was standing down in the hole. And I guess the bomb explosion, the concussion, the blast—with rocks and sand—it hit my head. From there, I never know what happened. I was unconscious.

And from there, they found me in the hole. And they took me out—my buddy, I guess, the bodyguard. Probably told them I was unconscious, still alive. From there they took me back maybe about 300 yards, back to the water. They put me on a ship or aircraft carrier.

And people were all laying on folding cots. And when I got … immediately I jumped off the cot, and I don't know how I got to—they said I was staggering because mentally I was, you know, I was not normal. And I started running, they said. And, uh, they said I was running, going this way, hollering, you know. I don't know what all I said, but they caught up with me, I imagine, over there. They brought me back, told me to take it easy. I laid down. That was that. And the next day, some officers group make their rounds, you know. They told me, they said, "You are in no condition to go back to duty," he said. "We're going to send you back to the United States."

Chester Nez:

So we finally got close to the airport, tried to surround the airstation. It took us about almost three weeks to get that airport. And the Marines surrounded the area, and the other platoon and battalion, they took off beyond the airport. I was right close to the middle of the airport, that's where we stayed. And most of the time (about 95% of the time), [we] keep that radio going, sending messages, receiving messages—what they need: supplies of all different kinds, ammunition, bombs, medical supplies, food; just about anything that they wanted. And that keeps coming in, going and going, and coming and going.

A hit on the gas dump, Peleliu Airfield, September 1944.
Photo courtesy National Archives.

Navajo Code Talkers on Bougainville. Front row, left to right: Earl Johnny, Kee Etsicitty, John V. Goodluck, David Jordan. Back row, left to right: Jack C. Morgan, George H. Kirk, Tom Jones, Henry Bahe Jr.

Photo courtesy National Archives.

REST & RELAXATION

Chester Nez:

The only time where we used to hear good music in those days is when we come back to rest area, called a rest area. Come back to spend maybe two, three weeks, do what you want, stuff like that, you know. And they send you off again.

What kind of music did you listen to back then?

Like Lombardo, uh—what's his name?—Benny Goodman, Nat King Cole, some of those guys that used to play mostly dance music. Entertainment. They used to put up these big speakers, you know, way up in the palm trees, coconut trees. They used to play that music real loud, man!

Kee Etsicitty:

On Guadalcanal, we used to box. We don't get nothing, we just want to do it. You know, you got nothing else to do. You know, you want to show that you're tougher than the other guy. Maybe that's the idea. So one day, I box away. Then the guy told us, "Hey, you're 112 pounds. There's another guy that wants to fight." OK, I'll take it. So, without warming up, I got in the ring with the guy. Yeah, the first round, that's his. Hit me all over my head and my body, everything. He was good. Second time, I kind of got warmed up, so I hit him back, three or four times. The third round, that was mine. Hell, he was easy. I do a lot of jabbing. But he won. There was a couple of, three guys that were standing right over there. And they're looking, watching the show. I went over there and talked to these guys, and one of them came close to me. He said, "You know what, chief?" he said (well, you know, in the service, everybody's "chief," any Indian is "chief," they call you "chief"), he said, "You know what, chief? Next time you're going to go box like that, warm up real good. Warm up yourself, shadow box. You done real good in the third round," he said. "If you warmed up before you got in the ring, you would have got that thing sewed up right then," he said. He's kind of a slim guy. And I asked him "Do you box, too?" He nod his head and said "Yeah, that's what I do for a living." He said, "My name is Barney Ross," he said. He was the welterweight champion of the world one time; was in the Marine Corps. He knew what he was talking about. "You know what you're doing, but you're slow."

Chester Nez:
They told us that morning, ready to board ship to hit the Iwo Jima. And that morning everybody boarded ship, all my division boarded ship. And we were ready to get on the landing craft, and there was a guy coming around; he had a pad, calling out some names. And my name was on that list. And he says, "PFC Chester Nez." "Hey, I'm over here." And he came over and he told me, he says, "You're going home." I was really lucky. And he said "get your gear and get your stuff together and wait here. They'll pick you up."

So I got aboard ship and said we're going home. So we left. It took us a little over three weeks to reach San Francisco. The Golden Gate Bridge—we went right under that.

5

Iwo Jima

A lot of these Marines, you can see them out there, floating around. Try to ask for help … and these guys were drowning. That's where a lot of them died, I know.
—Kee Etsicitty

American flag on top of Mount Suribachi, Iwo Jima.
Photo courtesy National Archives.

Samuel Tso:

After the practice at Saipan, it's always sometime at night we move out. That night, sometime towards morning I notice we were heading north. The next two days, about afternoon, the sea got rough. Boy, all the Marines got seasick. And myself, I got seasick. I went up to the top deck and heaved all that food I ate. When I heaved, got seasick, all that breeze from the ocean—I can smell fish. It feels so good, feels so good. It relieves my seasickness. I looked to the right and to the left. All of these ships were going forward: battleships, transport surface … cruisers and all that. And I say, oh my gosh, with this much help we'll overrun that little island in one day.

Approaching Iwo Jima, February 19, 1945.
Photo courtesy National Archives.

Keith Little:

Usually on landing day, on D-Day, usually it's four o'clock in the morning, three or four o'clock in the morning—call for chow. And a lot of guys will tease each other. "Are you enjoying your last meal? Well, you eat lots." "You're going to get sick in the landing boat and throw it back out anyway, so why eat?" Crazy things like that, crazy jokes that makes you wonder.

Samuel Tso:

February 19, 1945: that's the first time I saw Iwo Jima. Artillery guns from big ships pounding that island. All that dust and smoke. I think, looking over there, how can anybody live through that? Sometime in the morning there, on February 19th, we land there. There were no shots. So I figured that all that shelling and bombing, it killed all the Japanese. When we landed and went on top of the sand dunes, *that's* when they opened up fire. They let us land first, and then they opened fire on us.

Bill Toledo:

We landed there; there was three divisions that landed there. The first two divisions was 4th and 5th; landed first. The 3rd was the floating reserves, you know—were out floating around while those guys were fighting. And then about four days later we landed to help them out. What happened was, they figured that we'll take the island in about little over a week, 'cause they were bombing it for over 30 days and shelling it with ships, battleships, and cruisers.

And then they landed. And then after they landed, they start advancing into the island, inland. And this is out in the open now, it's not jungle anymore. There's a big volcano called Mt. Suribachi. From a certain angle it looks like a hogan, you know, round like this. But behind it, it's all hollow-like, it's a crater. Anyway, what happened was these Japanese had dug tunnels underneath the island, connecting tunnels. When they were shelling it on the top, they were all underground. Didn't hurt them. So, so when the Marines landed, they started advancing into the inland. They came out, out of the tunnels and the caves, you know. They start taking advantage of these Marines when they're out in the open. You can see them clearly, you know. These guys have no place to hide, you know. They're out in the open. The sand's about that deep. Black sand, you know, volcano sand: it's hard to walk on, it's hard to drive on. So we lost a lot of men that first day, first few days.

Alfred Newman:

When we got there … it was still dark. We could just see the fire from the big guns, and I guess the Japanese were returning fire. As we came closer and closer, the whole island was just covered with smoke, gunpowder smoke.

And, uh, 'course we had to get off the ship, get aboard those landing boats; and the sea was a little rough. It was kind of hard— you just have to time yourself when it comes back up, and get down at the bottom of the net. It's a rope like that, and there are lines like this and this, little squares, and you step in those little squares and hang onto the one that's going up and down. It's just like a ladder. So just have to watch it. When the water's rough, some guys miss it. The boat would hit the ship, bounce back, and guys drop down in the water—have to fish them out. Or they miss the whole thing. Some just fall in. You really had to watch it. You just kind of time yourself. You could see the boat go down, and as it rises, you just, just make sure you're almost at the bottom of the part where the boat will be—then just jump off, land in the boat.

Troops go over the side of a transport
Photo courtesy National Archives.

Anyway, it takes, it takes hours to get, to get all the troops off. All the boats would be circling, all the landing boats would be circling around up there, waiting until a whole battalion is off the boat, maybe two or three battalions, and then they all fall in line like this, you know, and just head straight for the beach, nothing to stop them, they just go. You hear people praying, Catholics, I don't know what other religions. You could tell the Catholics praying because they go like this, mumble to themselves. And others, they just shut their eyes. And the closer you get to the shore, you … with all that firing going on, bombing going on, they still … Japanese had a chance to do their shoot. See shells falling amongst the boats. If you're unlucky, your boat gets hit, and then you're either wounded or dead.

And when we hit the beach, all the equipment was just all bogged down in the sand, the trucks especially. And some of the boats I guess were hit, and they were just useless. They were all just clutter on the beach. We're all trying to run ashore. I guess we were on the second wave, I guess, 'cause the beach was crowded. The landing beach was about, I don't know, maybe two miles. But where we landed, it was crowded—I mean, broken equipment and, and corpsmen bringing dead, wounded out. They left the dead on the beach; they didn't bother with them. They're dead. Trying to save all the living ones. See guys with no arms, no legs, maybe part of the body shot off; some guys just, just laying face down, just the way they were hit, never move.

Kee Etsicitty:
Lot of these Marines died there, I know. They were alive. They are floating around. They need help. They didn't have no help. They don't have no corpsmen. They don't have no doctor. They can't turn around and back, take them to the flag shore hospital ship 'cause you can't turn around. It was crowded, it was already, everything was all shot up; it's like a junkyard, all the way down. A lot of these Marines, you can see them out there, floating around. Try to ask for help … and these guys were drowning. That's where a lot of them died, I know.

Alfred Newman:
And, uh, while we were trying to climb this sandy beach, it was kind of steep. It was real sandy. You know how sand is: you try to climb it, you just slide back down. Edmund Henry and I were just trying our best to get up there, and there was — heard those shells coming. There was a great big ol' hole there, in the sand. We all jumped in there, and about five or six guys right on top of us. Then about two or three minutes later we all started laughing, start crawling out of there. So we were pinned down for about one day there; couldn't move, had to spend the night on the beach there, just hoping that we that don't get hit with a shell or something.

The next morning, that's when we took off. We only went about maybe 100 yards or a little more. And, uh, fire was started again, so we had to stop and dig in, and just wait. We were there for about a week and they couldn't get supplies to us, food or anything because the Japanese were just playing heck with the people there, with supplies and stuff. They had the advantage from the mountain there; you could see what's going on on the beach. They had people way back on the side of the island, aiming their guns, their artillery.

Keith Little:
So they pull us back out of the fighting line, back a ways where we can be safe, have a little rest, and get a hot shower. So we went back, oh, maybe about half a mile — I guess what looked like a secure place. Told us to bivouac there. So here we're laying around resting. A sergeant comes around: "We'll have a hot shower pretty soon.

They're bringing it up." That hot shower really sounds good, and you never had coffee for all the time you're up at the front. And me and my buddy, we're, "by golly I hope we get hot coffee."

Pretty soon, here comes the jeep pulling a trailer. Parked it a ways from us, told us to get our mess kit ready, so we got ... picked up our mess kit, washed them up a little bit, washed the dirt off. And a lot of guys, they ran right up there and got right in line. Somehow, for some reason, I dragged my feet. Just about the time that I was getting to the chow

Marines unload rations from a tractor drawn trailer, Iwo Jima. February 29, 1945
Photo courtesy National Archives.

line, we heard that whistling, crazy noise coming. (I don't know what we call this ... the crazy shell, you know, they call them because you can see them going around or wobbling around, and you don't know where its going to go. Sometime it starts falling ... a lot of times it just falls a short ways from where they're firing.) And we heard it coming, and soon as we heard it, I ran right back down into the hole.

Right on our chow wagon! Blew up all of the food, plus wounded several guys there. And we never got to eat.

Alfred Newman:

On one of our advances we had to cross the airfield where it's just flat, nothing, nothing to hide behind. We had to run across there. Those Japanese just laid mortar shells, artillery, those big heavy machine guns. We just prayed silently and just dash across. When the firing gets heavy, just lay as flat as you can to the ground. You hear people screaming and crying and asking for help. There's nothing you could do about it, especially if you're not a corpsman. Especially out in the open like that, you just .... They tell you, "Keep moving, keep going."

Samuel Tso:

Why they called on us is beyond me. We were already at the front line with the other Marines, and yet they pulled us out of there from the front line. They took us over to the place called Death Valley. There's two hills with the same number, but one is "A" and the other one is "B." I don't really remember which one it was. I believe it's A. After we pulled out of the front line, I heard the officer say, "You will do your duty today." Our duty is to infiltrate the enemy line and operate behind it. So he marched us over to this hill 368. And then we looked and there it is, Death Valley. "You're going to run across that Death Valley right at noontime. When you cross the Death Valley over on the other side, look for Japanese machine gun nests. As soon as you locate it run back and report here." All kind of rocks and boulders are here. So they told us to go and line up here. And me and another Marine, a white guy—I don't really remember that guy's name—we went and took the last one over here. When they signal us at noontime, we're supposed to run across in zigzagging form.

So we start out. Just as soon as we cleared all these boulders, we ran into a whole bunch of Marines that got shot down, lying on top of each other. Some of them are still alive and they said, "Help." And my buddy and I, we stopped and tried to help one, and the sergeant screamed at us, "Complete your mission!" And so we took off and we ran straight into a machine gun nest. To my surprise he didn't fire. We could have been cut down like those Marines that were cut down. All I remember is, I guess my buddy … he threw a hand grenade. As soon he threw the hand grenade, we beat it back to hill #368. We ran back over here, and all the rest ran back over here. And there, some of them found machine gun nests too. And we found the one over here. So they came back over here and reported, and they put it on the map. And while we were trying to tell the guy that my buddy was put over there, they pulled me aside and the sergeant really … "Goddamit Chief, don't you know how to take orders yet? That was not your duty to try to help those Marines. Those are the guys that are going to go help them right now. They're specially trained for that." Boy, he was chewing me out!

But as soon as the location of the machine gun was known, they ordered artillery fire, mortar fire, and rockets right on these targets. Within five minutes you could see all the rockets going; and then the mortars going up, coming down, and the artillery's blasting away. All hell broke loose on that machine gun nest! That place was pulverized by all those shells. Within about 20 or 30 minutes they stopped firing.

When all the dust and flying debris still flying, they ordered the Marines across. I just sat there and looked over there. They just walked across completely without any fire. And then the officer says, "Mission accomplished. Recon company, you had enough. Go back to the ship." Oh, that was the best news I ever had.

Bill Toledo:
Sometimes we have wounded men, and they had to use all available men to go and get these guys in. And … and I don't know how we lost each others, me and Richard. He's supposed to be watching me! [laughs] He was one of those guys that was a trackman, you know. Real fast, you know. He'd go and run out there and bring somebody in and runs back again. And I'd go out there and help these guys. Me and another guy were moving this wounded guy across the airfield. The Japanese are using mortar … mortar shells, you know, it's a small, it's a small … a small, uh… I think they're 16 millimeter mortar, where they feed them from the top and they shoot up in the air like this, and shoot quite a ways. And then they have the bigger one they call a 90 millimeter. It's real wicked. You can hear when they comes in, you can hear that whistling, you know. You better get out of the way when you hear that coming! And they used to use rockets, too, on that island, on that north side. You could hear that screeching noise.

Anyway, me and another guy, we went …we went to get this wounded guy on a stretcher. He got hit—the guy that was helping got hit. And the guy that was on the stretcher, he was screaming, you know, because he was really hurting. And I was dragging him by myself into the back of the airfield, drag him in there and unload him there, just roll him off the stretcher; took the stretcher back over there where this guy was, and roll him on there; brought him in. So everybody was helping bringing these wounded guys in, and Richard was out running around. He said he lost me that night. Finally I guess he showed up, and he said, "Oh my God, I'm glad he's alive." He sobbed when he saw me.

Samuel Tso recalls a very vivid, extraordinary dream:

A lot of times some of the Navajo people say, "Weren't you scared?" I say, "Yes I was scared."

But one night I was asleep. That night I was dreaming about an Indian Maiden. I can still picture it: her hair dripped down, all down, almost to her knees; wearing a buckskin coat, and she said, "Here, take this and wear it, and you will come back to us." I was dreaming then, and when I was dreaming that I was reaching for it, and I was saying something to her. And I guess that's the time my buddy kicked me and woke me up, and he says, "Hey, Sam, are you having a nightmare?" It was so real that I just got up and sat at the edge of the foxhole, thinking about it. After a while they went for breakfast. All of them went over there. I just sat there, thinking about my dream. When they came back, they saw me still sitting there. And they asked me, "Hey, Chief! Are you still there? What's the matter?" I think all I said was, "Oh, I'm thinking." I didn't bother to talk about it. And after a while they had a mail call. You see, I never go to a mail call because my father and my mother and the rest of them, they don't know how to read and write. I wrote to them, but I never received any letter. They went to the mail call. After awhile there was a guy running back, and he lifts up a letter and says, "Hey Chief! You got a letter, you got a letter!" Came running, came close to me, and all of a sudden he says, "There's something in it." So when he brought it to me, and as soon as I got the letter, I look at the return address. Nothing. So we open the letter, pull it out ... Oh my gosh! That dream ... in my dream ... the thing she was handing me to wear—it's in that letter! "Hey, I'm supposed to wear this." So I put it on my neck. As soon as I put it on my neck, all fear dissipated. All I could say was, "I'm going home. I'm going home."

Mail unloaded at Motoyama Airfield No. 1, Iwo Jima. 1945.
Photo courtesy National Archives.

What was it exactly?

That's a ... do you know Juniper berries? The seeds inside it, made into a Catholic rosary—that's what I got.

Did it come with a letter?

No note or anything. Just laying there, and in my dream I was told to wear it.

So you received no letters in the service except that one?

That's the only one. After the war I looked and tried to find who the person is. I never found her.

Alfred Newman:

Edmund Henry got a letter that was already two ... three weeks old, 'cause you don't get mail every day when you're in combat—maybe once a week, or something like that, whenever you can … are able to get the mail up there. Anyway he came back and we sit in the tent and he asked me, he said, "Did you know that your mother passed away?" I said, "No, I didn't know." Whether it was his cousin or someone that wrote to him — she worked in a hospital over in Rehoboth; that's where my mother was operated on. And she died there. So … almost three weeks when I heard about it; then I, uh … I didn't say anything. I just walk out the tent and walked a couple of hundred yards away, and sat there and just thought about it. And I just figured well, there's nothing I could do about it. It's too bad. Well, before I left she told me, she said before we left, on the way back to San Diego after the training, when we parted, she told me, she said *"Doo shii naa shiideeltesťda"* ["You probably won't see me again"] she said to me. I guess she knew she was ill, but I didn't know she was that bad.

    But she knew, huh?

    She knew. *"Aadoo adinini shima. Naashíídeeltseťshíí."* ["Don't say that, mother. You will probably see me again"]. Well, we just said our good-byes. That was it.

    Then later they said, "You got a telegram in the Red Cross tent," they told me. So I went over there, and they say, "Here's a telegram." I guess they read it. They said, "It's about your mother passing away." I said, "What do you mean?" I said, "I heard about that two weeks ago," I said. I was disgusted with them. I don't know how long they had it, but maybe it just got there that day, or whatever. So I just walked out of there, didn't say no more. I wrote home and asked them; they said well, we sent a telegram there right away, the next day, or I don't know when … of course mail was slow in those days, there was no Priority. There was a big war going on, you know, you couldn't pick out certain one to do favors, you know, not unless you lost both legs or two arms or something like that; they ship you right back. So that's how I heard about that. And then, that's what I did, I … didn't really worry about anything. I just figured when I got home, everything will be all different.

Kee Etsicitty:

    You know, in the evening from Tokyo (you can hear it on Iwo Jima), there's a young lady that went to school at UCLA, she graduated from UCLA; she, her family's in Tokyo. She's a well educated lady. Her name was Tokyo Rose, they call her. She used to talk to everybody. She say your girlfriend or your wife is running around with somebody else. She's good at that.

Bill Toledo:

    The island is just about …I'd say about eight square miles. Tiny island. It took 36 days to take that island. And we lost quite a bit of men there, you know. We're … the 3rd Division was the last to move out, in March. That's when — while we're over there, we lost our president, you know, Roosevelt. We lost him during around Easter, we lost him. So that's when President Truman took over.

Shell shot trees with Mt. Suribachi in the distance.
Photo courtesy National Archives.

6

The War Ends

People heard the news; yelling, shooting, and sirens going off. "What happened?" "The Japanese surrendered!" they said. "Break out the beers!"
— Alfred Newman

Navajo Code Talker Samuel Sandoval beneath a pagoda, Okinawa, 1945.
Photo courtesy National Archives.

Kee Etsicitty:

One day, there was an old white haired guy come up here, walked through there. He was an officer, Naval officer. I says, "Aye, aye sir. Hello, sir." He walked away, stood right there, and turned around. He said, "Young man, how are you?"

"I'm all right sir."

"Now that the war is just about over," he said, "I'd like for someone to call me by my first name," he says. He says, "My name is Chester W. Nimitz." He's an admiral.

He was walking … I just salute, said, "Aye, aye, sir," and then went back there.

Bill Toledo:

Anyway, we moved off the island and move back to Guam. We had a rest day, and start training again. And this time they told that us we were going to land on the mainland of Japan, all six Marine divisions. So we were training.

Alfred Newman:

We went back to Guam, go back to Guam for the next … prepare for the next invasion. In the meantime I guess they took Peleliu and Okinawa and while we were on Guam getting new recruits, new training. And we were supposed to hit the southern end of Japan sometime in November. We were all getting ready for that on Guam.

While some of the troops went to Guam, others were sent to Okinawa, which was invaded on April 1, 1945.

Alfred Peaches:

And we went around on the shoreline—this was at nighttime. So we came around and attacked from behind. And that night, we turned around, going with the troops again, going forward again. And the night fell just before … there was a hill, rocky area. It was, there was a bunch of what they call tomb … concrete … we didn't know what it was. All over the hill, on the hillside. We couldn't dig it in, for foxholes to stay in overnight. So we tried to open that, those concrete things, and we opened one, and there was a body — it was a graveyard; they stored bodies in there. And the

Marines pinned down by enemy sniper fire on Cemetery Ridge in Okinawa, June 1, 1945. The Navajo Code term for "cemetery" is `jish-cha`, *or "among devils."*
Photo courtesy National Archives.

only place was to stay overnight was in that thing. So we took the bodies out of there and set it outside. And we used it for headquarters overnight. That's what we did. That's what happened.

Kee Etsicitty was on the island of Tinian in the late summer of 1945:

The intelligence officers, you know, just like I said, they think out loud sometimes. There's a big bomb. We talked to each other, us Navajos, about that thing. We just called it a big, powerful bomb. That's all. We didn't say "atomic bomb": we didn't know. So this is a big, powerful bomb. It's going to Japan. So it's waiting right out there, you know. A few days later, I guess, they took off and dropped the bomb on Nagasaki.

The first atomic bomb was dropped on Hiroshima on August 6, 1945, the second was dropped on Nagasaki three days later. On August 14, Japan surrendered.

Keith Little:

Our radio shack was down at the end of the street and it's manned 24 hours a day. Sometimes we take our turns, everybody takes a turn manning the radio station. And one night about three o'clock in the morning, I imagine, we were all sound asleep. And here's this guy running down the street. "Hey! Hey! Hey you guys! Wake up! Wake up! The war is over!"

Somebody got the nerve to get out the door and tell the guy, "Will you shut up, you sonofabitch. Don't you know we're sleeping?"

"Really! Really! Come on down to the radio shack! Listen in. There's a broadcast being made from Washington, D.C. that says the war may be over. The war is over!" he says. So we went down there and listened in … the sleepyheads, you know barely listening. Then the radio says, "The empire of Japan is offering unconditional surrender," really clear. And the sleepyheads went wild from there.

Bill Toledo:

I was in San Diego. I was … I think I was U.S.O., you know, where all the veterans come for entertainment in downtown San Diego. U.S.O.—that's where I was that afternoon when I heard the news. That afternoon, you know, all … it was in the middle of town … the traffic stopped. Everybody came out in the street, honking their horns, people hugging each others. And I guess that happened all over the country. And that was a big celebration. Everybody was just hugging strangers, all down the streets, everybody hollering. It was something. It was some big news. So just imagine what happened in these big cities, you know, in that year. It wasn't long after that, I got discharged.

Alfred Newman:

We were on Guam in August. Sometime at night around nine, ten o'clock, something like that, the siren went off, gunfire went off. I guess people heard the new; yelling, shooting and sirens going.

"What happened?"

"The Japanese surrendered!" they said. "Break out the beers!"

Yeah, everybody wanted to drink beer, but the commanding officer said no. No way. People go wild when they get drunk; they'd probably shoot one another and all that. He knew. By morning everybody was smiling and it was just quiet. "When are we going home?"

7

Going Home

That was the happiest time I remember.
— Alfred Peaches

Monument Valley, Arizona.
Photo by Courtney Mack

Alfred Newman:

It was early December when we got aboard one of these LST's, real slow tugboats (it seemed like, anyway). I think there were four of them. We're all crammed in there, and started for Hawaiian Islands. Took us two weeks to get to Hawaiian Islands from Guam. And, about almost a week out of Hawaiian Islands, we ran out of food. There was no more food. It just so happened that some other LST had extra food, only they were rations—little Cracker Jack box things; they had can of sausage, a can about that high, about that big around; cheese sticks; two cigarettes; a couple of sticks of gum—that was it, that was our meal for the day, until we hit the Hawaiian Islands.

Bill Toledo:

When I was getting discharged, after I got … signed everything, and I was going out the door, the colonel called me back. "Hey, Toledo," he said, "I want you to keep your mouth shut about what you went through, about the code you that used in the war. Keep your mouth shut. Don't tell anybody, not even your family, or your buddies. Anybody. It might be used again," he said. So that was what I was told. So I kept my mouth shut for about … until 1982. And the code was declassified in 1968, I think.

Alfred Newman:

And about the second day out, we all went to, went to sleep. And the next morning we woke up and, boy, that ship was just rocking like this, just like a cork. It would go up and then down. Them waves, they were higher than the ship, great big waves. We hit a cyclone, I guess, in the ocean. That ship was just like a cork. It would go one way this way, and then the other. Go on underneath a big wave, and just cover the whole thing, the deck. And just before breakfast, the sergeant that was in charge of us, he says "Everybody up for roll call!" And here we go, hardly standing up on the deck, with the waves coming over like that, calling our names to say "Here." We're all facing the sergeant; guess a great big ol' wave behind us came over and just swept us across the ship's deck, just like ten pins. I hit the side of the ship where the steel ladders were, with my leg right here, just busted right here, boom. Some of the guys had a … one guy had a dislocated arm, one guy had a cut on his head. Good thing the ship had a … a—what do they call it?—not a railing, but a steel thing running along the edge, about that high; then on top of that was two cables running along the edge of the ship. This one guy—I guess we all thrown against … I got thrown against the steel ladder. That's where I got hung up on it. I just happened to see one guy float like this all the way back to the fan tail of the ship. After it was all over, the roll call was over by then, we all got back into where our quarters, everybody was laughing, joking; and everybody seen one another, what was happening to them, how they were floating across the ship.

And we just sat there, and about noontime: "Chowtime." And this time they had a rope from our area to the mess hall, a great big ol' rope that we could hold on to get to the mess hall. And the storm was still going. And we got down in there, down in there on the lower deck where the dining hall was. And that was a mess! There was sandwiches and whatever—fruit, there was a dessert; it was all on the ground, all on the floor, on the deck. One guy was carrying coffee pot, coffee, and the ship went this way; he just went like that, sailing. He spilled that coffee on himself. Another guy was carrying a tray. He couldn't stand up, he had to let it go and keep himself from falling hard on the deck. There was coffee, milk, you name it. Whatever they were giving for food, it's all on the ship's deck. They told us, "Go back to your quarters. We'll give you sandwiches." So we all went back and came up with a sack of sandwiches that they gave us and we ate that way. That's the way we had our noon meal.

Samuel Tso:

And I came back—finally got discharged in March 29, 1946. I had trouble getting home. I bought bus ticket all the way to Gallup. The bus I was riding only went to Winslow. From there, instead of waiting for the next bus, I hitchhiked out of there. Found out a guy from New York City, pick me up but he wanted to go visit Petrified National Forest first. We came back and he decided to eat at that park restaurant. We sat down there, and here I was really wanting to go home. We sat down to eat and to my surprise he ordered two beers. And the guy working there, he says, "I'm not serving that Indian any beer." And my guy that I caught a ride, he got kind of sore about it. "Why not? He fought for his country and yet you don't even serve him!" And they got into a real argument over it. So the other guy finally gave in and he says "OK, you'll be responsible for him." So then he finally brought a beer there and we had beer with our meals. I think all he said was, "For crying sake, what kind of a state is this?" or something like that. But he gave me a ride to Gallup. I got off there and he went on.

I had to stay overnight and catch the mail truck the following day back to Chinle. From Chinle to my home it's about 20 or 25 miles.

Samuel Tso hitchhiked from there. He found a man able to give him a ride. But first, work had to be finished on his automobile.

He's there with his Model T Ford. And he was sitting there in the shade, and the two ladies were repairing tires. And then I found out that those are his wives. He had two wives there. They repaired the tires. He put me on and took me about 50 miles to Many Farms. From Many Farms, I have to go to Black Mountain. There's no road, just cow trails. So I took out my sea bag and I walk about half a mile. And I hid my sea bag again, right there. Otherwise I would have tote that sea bag all the way—maybe 12 or 13 miles. But the sun was getting way down there so I had to hurry. I walk and walk and walk. I would say I walked about something like eight miles. Where I first saw my sister and my cousins came to the springs, I had to go through that route. I stopped and drank at that spring right on top and then on about another two miles there. There's a stack of rocks. On that stack of rocks on the south side they usually hide mirrors underneath there. So I looked around under the rocks and then I found it. From there I flashed sunlight back to where my parents camp—chief camp. I keep flashing until someone on a horseback came out and I stopped flashing, put the mirror back underneath the rock, and I walked and meet him. And it was my brother. So we went on home.

When I got home, I found out my mother, my father, and my sister—my younger sister (we used to herd sheep together)—died. They're no longer. Only my older sister and her family living there. And where I was born—and I thought that's my land—somebody else's already living there. So I just couldn't bear to be there anymore. I just stayed there overnight.

The next morning just at dawn, I just got up, took a drink of water, and walk off. And I walked off—I was determined to find my, my sister that went to school. All I know is I found out she's living somewhere in San Francisco. They don't have the address, but they know that she's over in San Francisco. So I started about a mile—my brother came up with the horse again and asked where am I going. I just told him "Obviously I have nothing left there, so I'm just leaving. But first I got to find my sister and tell her that her mother and father are passed on, and our sister." So he says, "Here, take this horse. Take it to Chinle where the mail truck is. Leave the saddle and the bridle, all that there. Just put our names on there, and just release the horse. He'll come back over here," he says. So I rode the horse all the way to Chinle. Just when I got there the truck started out, so I had to stop the truck—told him I had to catch a ride back to Gallup. So I left the saddle and the blanket and then turned the horse loose there at the church, and get on the truck back to Gallup. Bought a bus ticket all the way to San Francisco.

Alfred Newman:

It was after New Year's when I got home. We got on the bus, the whole highway was new, was new to me; it was a narrow gravel road then, and this was all paved and wide. It was two lanes, but it was wide. And we got off the bus at Coolidge. There's a little Trading Post there, and, uh, this, this old lady and her husband—I knew them before I went to the service. And they looked at me and I told them who I, who I was. "Is that you?" they said to me.

"Yeah," I said, "it's me. I'm just getting home from the War," I said. "Can I leave my sea bag here?" I said. "I gotta walk across, I got no way of getting home; just by walking."

"Sure, leave it there," he said. So I left my, all my possessions there in the store with him and walked on. It's about maybe two to three miles I had to walk. I walk and I see all the familiar signs and all that, and just about, oh, I would say about two to three hundred yards from the home where I was going to, I saw my sister walking. She was going this way, I guess that she was going to chase me back or I don't know what she was going to do. She was looking down on the ground walking. I just kept walking, I didn't say anything, I just kept on walking. And she looked up and stared at me and, *"Shínaayí"* ["older brother"] she said. She come running, she come running; hugged each other and walked back to the house over there. She just said her mother's gone. "Yeah, I know about it," I said.

So I greeted the rest of the family. Of course my brothers weren't there—I guess they were in the service; and greeted my new stepmother. That was about it. No big celebration or nothing.

Chester Nez:

So I got back to San Diego and signed my discharge papers and they bought my ticket. [I] boarded a train and went back home to Gallup. And in Gallup everything was so quiet. There's nothing going on. So from there I hitchhiked. Got outside of town and hitchhiked. It took me almost a whole day to get back home.

And when I got back to the our trading post, the trader (this man, he's a white guy), he was really happy to see me. So he took my sea bag and threw it in his jeep and said "I'll take you home." It's not too far—about two miles, I guess, to my place. And he took me home, and he dropped me off about 100 yards from my place. He took my stuff out and he took off. And my sister was the first one that had … that … she came running to me. She was crying, really glad to see me. My dad wasn't home that day. He was out somewhere helping out some people, you know. He had some kind of medicine going on, you know, a sing. So everyone went back, pick up my sea bag and went back into the hogan. Everybody was happy to see me. I was so glad to be home. And then my dad, two or three days later, my dad came home and he was so happy to see me. So I stayed around home for two or three weeks. Finally they decided to get me a medicine man to do a good medicine sing over me, to cheer me up … Indian way, the good way.

8

Life After the War

[Being a Navajo Code Talker] was an act beyond the call of duty.
—Jack Jones

Photo taken at a parade in South Carolina, 2002.
Front seat: Alfred Peaches
Back seat, left to right: Terri Peaches (daughter), Jeanette Peaches (Alfred's wife), Janet Ross (granddaughter)
Photo courtesy Alfred Peaches.

Samuel Tso made it back to San Francisco to tell his sister about the death of their parents and other sister. He had to find a job there to pay his way back to Fort Defiance, Arizona.

Then when I got back over there and stop by my cousin at Fort Defiance, and they said, "They've been looking for you." Then I found out there's a job waiting for me so I started working there. After I work about two weeks, they transferred me over to sanitorium hospital where there's a lot of Navajos with tuberculosis. And people that start working there, they don't want to work too long there because they're afraid of catching the tuberculosis. So I work there for a whole summer.

By August, they brought in a young girl to the sanitorium. The doctor examined her, and those people that—Navajos working there, they tried to translate what the doctors were saying. All this time there, I wonder how come the interviewer don't come right out and tell the parents what the doctor is saying? So I finally intervened and talked with the family. The doctor says, "The only chance she has is to inject air between the lung and the lung cavities. She has a 50-50 chance of living." So they gave him permission to do that. And sure enough, her lung burst. She, uh—blood fill up her lung and she died. After she died, the relatives came in and man, oh, man, the whole family were really mad at us. I said, "Why include me? I was just only interpreting what the doctors said." Because the Navajo believes all this … tribal belief, that you mention death before a person dies. And he said it, but I was interpreting it and I was included in that one. Boy, I really caught heck. By then I know why that other interpreter wasn't really interpreting what was said. And I was accused of bewitching that young lady's death there.

Bill Toledo:

And I decided to go back to school. See, I didn't finish high school. I only had eighth grade education when I went in. And I decided to go back to school, you know. That's what I really needed. We had this, they call it GI Bill of Rights, you know, that the government had offered to the serviceman. So I used that to go back to high school in Albuquerque. I finished high school in 1949.

Then I had two additional years in Kansas, north Kansas: Haskell [Institute, a college for American Indians]. Then after that I got married. I met my wife in high school. We knew each other about seven years before we got married.

Kee Etsicitty:

My dad said, "Why don't you go to the Ordnance and ask for a job?" So I went over there. And they hired me, no questions asked. I worked there as a … got a job there as a fork lift operator, unloading bombs and munitions that come in on box cars. Either that, or stacking ammunition in those igloos with a forklift; unloading bombs from the freight cars, stacking them outside bivouacs.

And that was my job for awhile. And then they transferred me into what they call surveillance— that was inspecting the ammunition; go around all those igloos, inspect them for deterioration or any faults that you might find. You reported that to the Chief Ammunition Inspector. And that was my job for I don't know how many years.

Samuel Tso attended classes at Utah State University:

There was another Navajo going to school there. So we started getting together and study together. And we always asked, "What would be the main point in these paragraphs?" Says you have to write down the main heading of the paragraph. He says fix it in your head and then search for the main point in there, as many main points as you can remember. So we start doing that, working together.

In the spring of my senior year, we just been reviewing and studying for our tests. I didn't go to bed until sometimes two o'clock in the morning. Wake up at six, just grab a cup of coffee and toast, head for school. When we got to school we had the same classroom to test. We walk in there, took a look at the test all the way through as fast as we could; see what the end says. So we looked through it and I found out that what we've been studying together, it's all in there. How we did was just go through it, as fast as we could. He and I were the first ones to leave the classroom. And the guys that finished came out and says, "What happened? Was it too hard for you?" I says, "No problem. We answered all of them." We go to the next one. Same thing ... we finish our test and went on home on Friday.

Saturday morning we went into town. People downtown come up to me and they ... congratulation. What are they congratulating me for? Do I have another son or something? And then, uh, the guy that runs the drugstore at Mac's Drug Store, he's real friendly to me. "Hey, Mac, what's the congratulation bit?"

"You mean you don't know?"

I say, "I don't know." He went over and picked up the newspaper. Right there: Two Native Americans on the honor roll. I couldn't believe it. I says, "I finally made it!"

Anyway, we finished with our school on Friday. And then I found out I got hired; start working the following Monday. I got hired over Many Farms High School and back over at Intermountain School. Many Farms found out that I wanted to work at Intermountain. Say, "We'll give you the next step in salary." So I told Intermountain they going to give me the next step in salary. "Oh, we'll do better." So I called back over there and told them they're going to give me a higher pay over there. "Oh, we'll beat that." And so ... and then Intermountain School says, "We'll give you one year's raise." OK, so I start working there. I worked there for 23 years.

By the 15th year, I was teaching, and teacher supervisor came in and evaluated my teaching. He just took all kinds of notes and left; and didn't bother to talk with me. Say you're doing this wrong, you do this, you should do it this way better—he didn't ever say anything. And then I was called in, and all of a sudden people congratulate me. And then they gave me a paper that says: Outstanding Teacher.

Bill Toledo:

I didn't even tell my wife or my kids about ... that I was a Code Talker, until one day when I was working day shift. My daughter and her mother were cleaning the bedroom, you know, dusting and all that. I had my service picture on my dresser. I had my discharge paper in the back of the picture. I guess somehow my daughter knocked that picture off the dresser and it landed on the floor, on the carpet. Part of the discharge paper came out. So she took it apart, you know, trying to straighten it out. She was looking at it and said, show it to her mother and said, "Hey, we have a Code Talker in the family!" That's how they found out.

And when I came back home, when I came from work that evening, they were at the door. "How come you didn't tell us?"

"Well, nobody ever asked me," I said.

Samuel Tso:

So I've been a teacher supervisor over at Lukachukai until July 15, 1983. I decided to retire. I decided to retire because I know one young lady. She's past retirement age but she keeps on, another year, another year. But when she did retire, I think she only live about six months and died. And I didn't want to have that to happen to me, so I retired July 15, 1983.

After that, what will I give the community here? Instead of running for leadership for the community, I decided to stay in with an educational field as a school board member.

You're still a school board member to this day? [9 July 2007]

Yeah. Right now I'm a school board member over at Many Farms. I think I only have a year and a half to go yet for high school, and I believe I want to call it a career there because my eyes failing me, my hearing's failing me. Especially my eyes; I found out I've got glaucoma.

Bill Toledo:

Got a job over there in the Anaconda Mining Company. They had their open pit over there by Paguate. I used to drive every day over there. I work over there about 30 years. I worked nine years for Anaconda, and then they laid me off, and I went to work for Homestake, just close by. I worked 20 years for Homestake, and that where I retired from in 1985. I lost my wife in 1985, just when I was retiring. She had all the plans for me, you know.

And after I retired in May of '85, I had a call from my adopted sister from Torreon. She was a teacher over there. She said, "I want you to come over here and make presentation to my students," she said. "It'll probably just take you about maybe 15 minutes," she said. OK. That was my first presentation. I went over there. I was talking to …from 1st graders to 8th graders, all day long. So I got started with this presentation stuff. From there, I go to different high schools, a lot of them in Albuquerque; and N[orthern] A[rizona] U[niversity], and Gallup and Tucson and Phoenix. All over the country. So I'm still doing that today.

Samuel Tso:

Right now I don't really know what to tell my grandchildren. The only thing I can tell them is to be loyal. Congress says you're a citizen of the United States now, and you have a right to free religion, you have a right to vote. A long time ago when I was a young man we were not allowed to vote. We were not even allowed to go into bars. Now we can go in there—but then, I don't recommend that for our young Navajo people. It is best for them to stay drug free. But with all the struggle they're going through, somewhere, sometime they will go into boozing around. I think that helps them forget a little bit, but then when it's all over you're still the same.

Jack Jones remembers back to his days as a Code Talker:

I would think … would say it is an act beyond the call of duty. It had protected a lot of our comrades from getting killed, just by sending messages.

Bill Toledo looks back at his accomplishments:

I'm really proud of myself that I took part in this program. And I always tell these Code Talkers, you know, that I think, I think we were put on this earth to do this for the country. And, "Yeah, I think so too," you know. We're picked out specially, pick us out to do this for the country, for our people, you know. I was always proud of myself that I did this for my people, for the country.

In 2001 the Navajo Code Talkers received Congressional Medals—Gold Medals to the First 29 or their descendants, and Silver Medals to the remaining Code Talkers. Jack Jones conversed with a fellow Code Talker who had incorporated his medal into a bolo tie:

I said, "Which side do you wear most?"

"Either side," he said. "All you have to do is turn one around like that. You can show this side, you can reverse it the other way," he said. Some fixed it that way.

What are they good for? Nothing. Nothing.

Kee Etsicitty:

You gotta have communication in a war. The Navajos were there, Navajo Code Talkers. I, you know, I just … sometimes you talk to the people like this, it chokes you, it makes you cry. Yeah, I cried before people, many times, talking like this. 'Cause there that makes you feel that you have done something for yourself, your family, for the government, for everybody, for the youngsters, people—this is what you help with. You help one, help them.

Samuel Tso:

I think we'll be better off as the years go along, that the people of America realize that we Native Americans *did* help during the World War. Thank you.

EPILOGUE

The returning Navajo veterans were changed by their wartime experiences, and in turn they forever changed the face of the Navajo Reservation. "I think it's we, the veterans of World War II," Keith Little asserts, "are the ones that brought the meaning of education back to our people, because a lot of us became leaders, became teachers, lawyers. Some became medicine men, community leaders—influential leaders around the reservation, even off the reservation."

The expansion of awareness from their wartime experiences brought about an increased awareness of prejudice. When the Navajo Code Talkers returned to the reservation, they were not even allowed to vote. Samuel Tso remembers that "I didn't really consider it being prejudiced against me. It's so much a part of life that it didn't bother me. But after I came back from the service, it really infuriated me." But change was in the air. By 1948, Navajos were finally allowed to vote. Over the next several decades, the bars and diners that had refused them service gradually ended their discriminatory behavior.

Given their history of harsh treatment by the federal government, given their constant encounters with racial prejudice, an obvious question is: why did the Navajos bother to go to war to defend the United States against a foreign aggressor? Often their reply is basically this—they did it to protect their homeland and their people. Samuel Tso explains, "Our reservation is part of the United States. Even the [Navajo] council delegates said go ahead and go join the service. 'You're doing this for your land and your people.' I said, 'that's worth fighting for,' so I joined. After I came back I found out we were doing this for the whole United States, the citizens of the United States."

"That is why it had to be done," says Keith Little, "to protect our land. So, in a sense, we really are patriotic, faithful to our country, to our land. See? That's why. We don't question it. If somebody invades the land in order to conquer the United States of America, they can be damn sure that the Navajos are going to be right there!"

The passage of time has given an aura to the participants of the Second World War: Franklin D. Roosevelt, Eisenhower, Patton, Nimitz now have the near-mythic resonance of Lincoln, Grant, Sherman, Robert E. Lee. With each passing day, the living memories of World War II fade a little more. Humanity's collective memory of this global struggle is preserved in the form of artifacts, written documents, photographs, films, sound recordings and—so long as there are people who lived through and can recall those days—remembrances. Many returning veterans were able to tell their stories when they got home. But the Navajo Code Talkers had to wait 23 years (until 1968) before they could tell anyone the true scope of their contribution.

Because their ancestors tenaciously held on to their way of life, the Navajo language and culture endures. This is the legacy of those who lived during the time of the Long Walk. Because of the Navajo Code Talkers' language, lives were saved, and the United States of America endures. This is the Code Talkers' legacy to humanity.

When I talk about it, it comes back to me.
Ahh … that's what I did.

— Kee Etsicitty

Appendix 1: The Navajo Code

This code, begun by the First 29 with a total of 211 words, was expanded as time progressed. The original word or letter is in the left column, followed by the Navajo Code Word, in italics, in the spelling invented by the Code Talkers—specifically, Wilsie Bitsie (one of the First 29) (McClain, Sally. "Navajo Weapon: The Navajo Code Talkers" Tucson: Rio Nuevo Pubishers [1981], p. 53). It is not the spelling used in the official Navajo orthographies. The third column contains English translations of the Navajo code words.

A	*wol-la-chee*	ant	L	*dibeh-yazzie*	lamb
	be-la-sana	apple		*ah-jad*	leg
	tse-nill	axe		*nash-doie-tso*	lion
B	*na-hash-chid*	badger	M	*tsin-tliti*	match
	shush	bear		*be-tas-tni*	mirror
	toish-jeh	barrel		*na-as-tso-si*	mouse
C	*moasi*	cat	N	*nesh-chee*	nut
	tla-gin	coal		*tsah*	needle
	ba-goshi	cow		*a-chin*	nose
D	*be*	deer	O	*a-kha*	oil
	chindi	devil		*tlo-chin*	onion
	lha-cha-eh	dog		*ne-ahs-jah*	owl
E	*ah-jah*	ear	P	*cla-gi-aih*	pant
	dzeh	elk		*bi-so-dih*	pig
	ah-nah	eye		*ne-zhoni*	pretty
F	*chuo*	fir	Q	*ca-yeilth*	quiver
	tsa-e-donin-ee	fly	R	*gah*	rabbit
	ma-e	fox		*dah-nes-tsa*	ram
G	*ah-tad*	girl		*ah-losz*	rice
	klizzie	goat	S	*dibeh*	sheep
	jeha	gum		*klesh*	snake
H	*tse-gah*	hair	T	*d-ah*	tea
	cha	hat		*a-woh*	tooth
	lin	horse		*than-zie*	turkey
I	*tkin*	ice	U	*shi-da*	uncle
	yeh-hes	itch		*no-da-ih*	Ute
	a-chi	intestine	V	*a-keh-di-glini*	victor
J	*tkele-cho-gi*	jackass	W	*gloe-ih*	weasel
	ah-ya-tsinne	jaw	X	*al-na-as-dzoh*	cross
	yil-doi	jerk	Y	*tsah-as-zih*	yucca
K	*jad-ho-loni*	kettle	Z	*besh-do-tliz*	zinc
	ba-ah-ne-di-tinin	key			
	klizzie-yazzie	kid			

ORGANIZATIONS

corps	*din-neh-ih*	clan
division	*ashih-hi*	salt
regiment	*tabaha*	edge water
battalion	*tacheene*	red soil
company	*nakia*	Mexican
platoon	*has-clish-nih*	mud
section	*yo-ih*	beads
squad	*debeh-li-zini*	black sheep

OFFICERS

officers	*a-la-jih-na-zini*	headmen
commanding general	*bih-keh-he*	war chief
major general	*so-na-kih*	two stars
brigadier general	*so-a-la-ih*	one star
colonel	*atsah-besh-le-gai*	silver eagle
lt. colonel	*che-chil-be-tah-besh-legai*	silver oak leaf
major	*che-chil-be-tah-ola*	gold oak leaf
captain	*besh-legai-na-kih*	two silver bars
lieutenant	*besh-legai-a-lah-ih*	one silver bar
1st lieutenant	*besh-legai-a-lah-ih*	one silver bar
2nd lieutenant	*ola-alah-ih-ni-ahi*	one gold bar
commanding officer	*hash-kay-gi-na-tah*	war chief
executive officer	*bih-da-hol-nehi*	those in charge

COUNTRIES

Africa	*zhin-ni*	blackies
Alaska	*beh-hga*	with winter
America	*ne-he-mah*	our mother
Australia	*cha-yes-desi*	rolled hat
Britain	*toh-ta*	between waters
China	*ceh-yehs-besi*	braided hair
France	*da-gha-hi*	beard
Germany	*besh-be-cha-he*	iron hat
Iceland	*tkin-ke-yah*	ice land
India	*ah-le-gai*	white clothes
Italy	*doh-ha-chi-yali-tchi*	stutter
Japan	*beh-na-ali-tsosie*	slant eye
Philippines	*ke-yah-da-na-lhe*	floating island
Russia	*sila-gol-chi-ih*	Red Army
South America	*sha-de-ah-ne-hi-mah*	south our mother
Spain	*deba-de-nih*	sheep pain

AIRPLANES

airplanes	*wo-tah-de-ne-ih*	air force
dive bomber	*gini*	chicken hawk

torpedo plane	*tas-chizzie*	swallow
observation plane	*ne-as-jah*	owl
fighter plane	*da-he-tih-hi*	humming bird
bomber	*jay-sho*	buzzard
patrol plane	*ga-gih*	crow
transport	*atsah*	eagle

SHIPS

ships	*toh-dineh-ih*	sea force
battleship	*lo-tso*	whale
aircraft carrier	*tsidi-hey-ye-hi*	bird carrier
submarine	*besh-lo*	iron fish
mine sweeper	*cha*	beaver
destroyer	*ca-lo*	shark
transport	*dineh-nay-ye-hi*	man carrier
cruiser	*lo-tso-yazzie*	small whale
mosquito boat	*tse-e*	mosquito

MONTHS

January	*yas-nil-tes*	crusted snow
February	*atsah-be-yaz*	small eagle
March	*woz-cheind*	squeeky voice
April	*tah-chill*	small plant
May	*tah-tso*	big plant
June	*be-ne-eh-eh-jah-tso*	big planting
July	*be-ne-ta-tsosie*	small harvest
August	*be-neen-ta-tso*	big harvest
September	*ghaw-jih*	half
October	*nil-chi-tsosie*	small wind
November	*nil-chi-tso*	big wind
December	*kesh-mesh*	Christmas

VOCABULARY

abandon	*ye-tsan*	run away from
about	*wola-che-a-he-gahn*	ant fight
abreast	*wola-chee-be-yied*	ant breast
accomplish	*ul-so*	all done
according	*be-ka-ho*	according to
acknowledge	*hanot-dzied*	acknowledge
action	*ah-ha-tinh*	place of action
activity	*ah-ha-tinh-y*	action ending in y
adequate	*beh-gha*	enough
addition	*ih-he-de-ndel*	addition
address	*yi-chin-ha-tse*	address
adjacent	*be-gahi*	near
adjust	*has-tai-nel-kad*	adjust

advance	*nas-sey*	ahead
advise	*na-netin*	advise
aerial	*be-zonz*	stinger
affirmative	*lanh*	affirmative
after	*bi-kha-di*	after
against	*be-na-gnish*	against
aid	*eda-ele-tsood*	aid
air	*nilchi*	air
airdome	*nilchi-beghan*	airdome
alert	*ha-ih-des-ee*	alert
all	*ta-a-tah*	all
allies	*nih-hi-cho*	our friends
along	*wolachee-snez*	long ant
also	*eh-do*	also
alternative	*na-kee-go-ne-nan-dey-he*	second postition
ambush	*khac-da*	ambush
ammunition	*beh-eli-doh-be-cah-ali-tas-ai*	ammunition
amphibious	*chal*	frog
and	*do*	and
angle	*dee-cahn*	slanting
annex	*ih-nay-tani*	addition
announce	*beh-ha-o-dze*	announce
anti	*wol-la-chee-tsin*	ant ice
anticipate	*ni-jol-lih*	anticipate
any	*tah-ha-dah*	any
appear	*ye-ka-ha-ya*	appear
approach	*bi-chi-ol-dah*	moving to
approximate	*to-kus-dan*	approximate
are	*gah-tso*	large (big) rabbit
area	*haz-a-gih*	area
armor	*besh-ye-ha-da-di-teh*	iron protected
army	*lei-cha-ih-yil-knee-ih*	dog faces
arrive	*il-day*	came
artillery	*be-al-doh-tso-lani*	many big guns
as	*ahce*	ace
assault	*altseh-e-jah-he*	first striker
assemble	*de-ji-kash*	bunch together
assign	*bah-deh-tahn*	assign
at	*ah-di*	at
attack	*al-tah-je-jay*	attack
attached	*a-hid-day-tih*	attached
attempt	*bo-o-ne-tah*	try
attention	*giha*	attention
authenticator	*hani-ba-ah-ho-zin*	know about
authorize	*be-bo-ho-snee*	authorize
available	*ta-shoz-teh-ih*	available

baggage	klailh	baggage
banzai	ne-tah	fool them
barge	besh-na-elt	barge
barrage	besh-ba-wa-chind	barrage
barrier	bih-chan-ni-ah	in the way
base	bih-tsee-dih	foundation
battery	bih-be-al-doh-tka-ih	three guns
battle	da-ah-hi-dzi-tsio	battle
bay	toh-ah-hi-ghinh	bay
bazooka	ah-zhol	bazooka
be	tses-nah	bee
beach	tah-bahn	beach
been	tses-nah-nes-chee	bee nut
before	bih-tse-dih	prior
begin	ha-hol-ziz	commenced from
belong	tses-nah-snez	long bee
between	bi-tah-kiz	between
beyond	bilh-la di	down below
bivouac	ehl-nas-teh	brush shelter
block	da-day-thah	to stop, to close
bomb(s)	a-ye-shi	eggs
booby trap	dineh-ba-whoa-blehi	man trap
borne	ye-chie-tsah	born elk
boundary	ka-yah-bi-na-has-dzoh	boundary
bull dozer	dola-alth-whosh	bull sleep
bunker	tsas-ka	sandy hallow
but	neh-dih	but
by	be-gha	by
cable	besh-lkoh	wire rope
caliber	nahl-kihd	move around
camp	to-altseh-hogan	temporary place
camouflage	di-nes-ih	hid
can	yah-di-zini	can
cannoneer	be-al-doh-tso-dey-dil-don-igi	big gun operator
capacity	be-nel-ah	capacity
capital	tkah-chae	sweat house
capture	yis-nah	capture
carry	yo-lailh	carry
case	bit-sah	case
casualty	bih-din-ne-dey	put out of action
cause	bi-nih-nani	cause
cave	tsa-ond	rock cave
ceiling	da-tel-jay	seal
cemetery	jish-cha	among devils
center	ulh-ne-ih	center
change	thla-go-a-nat-zah	change

channel	*ha-talhi-yazzie*	small singer
charge	*ah-tah-gi-jah*	charge
chemical	*ta-nee*	alkali
circle	*nas-pas*	circle
circuit	*ah-heh-ha-dailh*	circuit
class	*alth-ah-a-teh*	class
clear	*yo-ah-hol-zhod*	clear
cliff	*tse-ye-chee*	cliff
close	*ul-chi-uh-nal-yah*	close
coast guard	*ta-bas-dsissi*	shore runner
code	*yil-tas*	peck
colon	*naki-alh-deh-da-al-zhin*	two spots
column	*alth-kay-ne-zih*	column
combat	*da-ah-hi-jih-ganh*	fighting
combination	*al-tkas-ei*	mixed
come	*huc-quo*	come
comma	*tsa-na-dahl*	tail drop
commercial	*nai-el-ne-hi*	commercial
commit	*huc-quo-la-jish*	come glove
communication	*ha-neh-al-enji*	making talk
conceal	*be-ki-asz-jole*	conceal
concentration	*ta-la-hi-jih*	one place
concussion	*whe-hus-dil*	concussion
condition	*ah-ho-tai*	how it is
conference	*be-ke-ya-ti*	talk over
confidential	*na-nil-in*	kept secret
confirm	*ta-a-neh*	make sure
conquered (conquer)	*a-keh-des-dlin*	won
consider	*ne-tsa-cas*	think it over
consist	*bilh*	consist
consolidate	*ah-hih-hi-nil*	put together
construct	*ahl-neh*	to make
contact	*ah-hi-di-dail*	come together
continue	*ta-yi-teh*	continue
control	*nai-ghiz*	control
convoy	*tkal-kah-o-nel*	moving on water
coordinate	*beh-eh-ho-zin-na-as-dzoh*	known lines
counter attack	*woltah-al-ki-gi-jeh*	counter act
course	*co-ji-goh*	course
craft	*ah-toh*	nest
creek	*toh-nil-tsanh*	very little water
cross	*al-n-as-dzoh*	cross
cub	*shush-yahz*	cub
dash	*us-dzoh*	dash
dawn	*ha-yeli-kahn*	dawn
defense	*ah-kin-cil-toh*	defense

degree	*nahl-kihd*	degree
delay	*be-sitihn*	deer lay
deliver	*be-bih-zihde*	deer liver
demolition	*ah-deel-tahi*	blow up
dense	*ho-dilh-cla*	wet
depart	*da-de-yah*	depart
department	*hogan*	dwelling, house
designate	*ye-khi-del-nei*	point out
desperate	*ah-da-ah-ho-dzah*	down to last
detach	*al-cha-nil*	detached
detail	*be-beh-sha*	deer tail
detonator	*ah-deel-tahi*	blow up
difficult	*na-ne-klah*	difficult
dig in	*le-eh-gade*	dig in
direct	*ah-ji-go*	direct
disembark	*eh-ha-jay*	get out
dispatch	*la-chai-en-seis-be-jay*	dog is patch
displace	*hih-do-nal*	move
display	*be-seis-na-neh*	deer is play
disposition	*a-ho-tay*	disposition
distribute	*nah-neh*	distribute
district	*be-thin-ya-ni-chi*	deer ice strict
do	*tse-le*	small pup
document	*beh-eh-ho-zinz*	document
drive	*ah-nol-kahl*	drive
dud	*di-giss-yahzie*	small dummy
dummy	*di-giss-tso*	big dummy
each	*ta-lahi-ne-zini-go*	each
echelon	*who-dzah*	line
edge	*be-ba-hi*	edge
effective	*be-delh-need*	effective
effort	*yea-go*	with all your might
element	*ah-na-nai*	troop representing others
elevate	*ali-khi-ho-ne-oha*	elevate
eliminate	*ha-beh-to-dzil*	eliminate
embark	*eh-ho-jay*	get on
emergency	*ho-nez-cla*	emergency
emplacement	*la-az-nil*	emplacement
encircle	*ye-nas-teh*	encircle
encounter	*bi-khanh*	go-against
engage	*a-ha-ne-ho-ta*	agreed
engine	*chidi-bi-tsi-tsine*	engine
engineer	*day-dil-jah-he*	fire builder
enlarge	*nih-tsa-goh-al-neh*	make big
enlist	*bih-zih-a-da-yi-lah*	written signature
entire (and all)	*ta-a-tah*	entire

entrench	*e-gad-ah-ne-lih*	make ditch
envelop	*a-zah-gi-ya*	envelop
equipment	*ya-ha-de-tahi*	equipment
erect	*yeh-zihn*	stand up
escape	*a-zeh-ha-ge-yah*	escape
establish	*has-tay-dzah*	set up
estimate	*bih-ke-tse-hod-des-kez*	estimate
evacuate	*ha-na*	evacuate
except	*neh-dih*	except
exchange	*alh-nahl-yah*	exchange
execute	*a-do-nil*	will happen
explosive	*ah-del-tahi*	explosive
expect	*na-wol-ne*	expect
expedite	*shil-loh*	speed up
extend	*ne-tdale*	make wide
extreme	*al-tsan-ah-bahm*	each end
fail	*cha-al-eind*	fail
failure	*yees-ghin*	failure
farm	*mai-be-he-ahgan*	fox arm
feed	*dzeh-chi-yon*	feed
field	*clo-dih*	outside
fierce	*toh-bah-ha-zsid*	afraid
file	*ba-eh-chez*	file
final	*tah-ah-kwo-dih*	that is all
flame thrower	*coh-ah-ghil-tlid*	flame thrower
flank	*dah-di-kad*	flank
flare	*wo-chi*	light streak
flight	*ma-e-as-zloli*	fox light
force	*ta-na-ne-ladi*	without care
form	*be-cha*	form
formation	*be-cha-ye-lailh*	formation
fortification	*ah-na-sozi*	cliff dwelling
fortify	*ah-na-sozi-yazzie*	small fortification
forward	*tehi*	let's go
fragmentation	*besh-yazzie*	small metal
frequency	*ha-talhi-tso*	big singer
friendly	*neh-hecho-da-ne*	friendly
from	*bi-tsan-dehn*	from
furnish	*yeas-nil*	furnish
further	*wo-nas-di*	further
garrison	*yah-a-da-hal-yon-ih*	take care of
gasoline	*chidi-bi-toh*	gasoline
grenade	*ni-ma-si*	potatoes
guard	*ni-dih-da-hi*	guard
guide	*nah-e-thlai*	guide
hall	*lhi-ta-a-ta*	horse all

half track	*alh-nih-jah-a-quhe*	race track
halt	*ta-akwai-i*	halt
handle	*bet-seen*	handle
have	*jo*	have
headquarter	*na-ha-tah-ta-ba-hogan*	headquarter
held	*wo-tah-ta-eh-dahn-oh*	held
high	*wo-tah*	high
high explosive	*be-al-doh-be-ca-bih-dzil-igi*	powerful shell
highway	*wo-tah-ho-ne-teh*	high way
hold	*wo-tkanh*	hold
hospital	*a-zey-al-ih*	place of medicine
hostile	*a-nah-ne-dzin*	not friendly
howitzer	*be-el-don-ts-quodi*	short big gun
illuminate	*wo-chi*	light up
immediately	*shil-loh*	immediately
impact	*a-he-dis-goh*	impact
important	*ba-has-teh*	important
improve	*ho-dol-zhond*	improve
include	*el-tsod*	include
increase	*ho-nalh*	increase
indicate	*ba-hal-neh*	tell about
infantry	*ta-neh-nal-dahi*	infantry
infiltrate	*ye-gha-ne-jeh*	went through
initial	*beh-ed-de-dlid*	brand
install	*ehd-tnah*	install
installation	*nas-nil*	in place
instruct	*na-ne-tgin*	teach
intelligence	*ho-ya*	smart
intense	*dzeel*	strength
intercept	*yel-na-me-jah*	interecpt
interfere	*ah-nilh-khlai*	interfere
interpret	*ah-tah-ha-ne*	interpret
invade	*a-tah-gi-nah*	moved into
investigate	*na-ali-ka*	track
involve	*a-tah*	involve
is	*seis*	seven
island	*seis-keyah*	seven island
isolate	*bih-tsa-nel-kad*	separate
jungle	*woh-di-chil*	jungle
kill	*naz-tsaid*	kill
kilocycle	*nas-tsaid-a-kha-ah-yeh-ha-dilh*	kill oil go around
labor	*na-nish*	labor
land	*kay-yah*	land
launch	*tka-ghil-zhod*	launch
leader	*ah-na-ghai*	leader
least	*de-be-yazie-ha-a-ah*	lamb east

leave	*dah-de-yah*	he left
left	*nish-cla-jih-goh*	left
left side	*nish-cla-jih-goh-na-nae-goh*	left side
less	*bi-oh*	less
level	*dil-konh*	level
liaison	*da-a-he-gi-eneh*	know other's action
limit	*ba-has-ah*	limit
litter	*ni-das-ton*	scatter
location (locate)	*a-kwe-eh*	spot
loss	*ut-din*	loss
machine gun	*a-knah-as-donih*	rapid fire gun
magnetic	*na-e-lahi*	pick up
manage	*hastni-beh-na-hai*	man age
maneuver	*na-na-o-nalth*	moving around
manufacturers	*besh-be-eh-el-ih-dih*	metal factory
map	*kah-ya-nesh-chai*	map
maximum	*bel-di-khon*	fill to top
mechanic	*chiti-a-nayl-inih*	auto repairman
mechanized	*chidi-da-ah-he-goni*	fighting cars
medical	*a-zay*	medicine
megacycle	*mil-ah-heh-ah-dilh*	million go around
merchant ship	*na-el-nehi-tsin-na-ailh*	merchant ship
message	*hane-al-neh*	message
military	*silago-keh-goh*	military
millimeter	*na-as-tso-si-a-ye-do-tish*	double mouse
mine	*ha-gade*	mine
minimum	*be-oh*	minimum
minute	*ah-khay-el-kit-yazzie*	little hour
mission	*al-neshodi*	mission
mistake	*o-zhi*	miss
mopping	*ha-tao-di*	mopping
more	*thla-na-nah*	more
mortar	*be-al-doh-cid-da-hi*	sitting gun
motion	*na-hot-nah*	motion
motor	*chide-be-tse-tsen*	car head
native	*ka-ha-teni*	native
navy	*tal-kah-silago*	sea soldiers
necessary	*ye-na-zehn*	want
negative	*do-ya-sho-da*	no good
net	*na-nes-dizi*	net
neutral	*do-neh-lini*	neutral
normal	*doh-a-ta-h-dah*	normal
not	*ni-dah-than-zie*	no turkey
notice	*ne-da-tazi-thin*	no turkey ice
now	*kut*	now
number	*beh-bih-ke-as-chinigh*	what's written

objective	*bi-ne-yei*	goal
observed	*hal-zid*	observed
obstacle	*da-ho-desh-zha*	obstacle
occupy	*yeel-tsod*	taken
of	*toh-ni-tkal-lo*	ocean fish
offensive	*bin-kie-jinh-jih-dez-jay*	offensive
once	*ta-lai-di*	once
only	*ta-ei-tay-a-yah*	only
operate	*ye-nahl-nish*	work at
opportunity	*ash-ga-alin*	opportunity
opposition	*ne-he-tsah-jih-shin*	opposition
or	*eh-do-dah-goh*	either
orange	*tchil-lhe-soi*	orange
order	*be-eh-ho-zini*	order
ordnance	*lei-az-jah*	under ground
originate	*das-teh-do*	begin
other	*la-e-cih*	other
out	*clo-dih*	out side
overlay	*be-ka-has-tsoz*	overlay
parenthesis	*atsanh*	rib
particular	*a-yo-ad-do-neh*	particular
party	*da-sha-jah*	party
pay	*na-eli-ya*	pay
penalize	*tah-ni-des-tanh*	set back
percent	*yal*	money
period	*da-ahl-zhin*	period
periodic	*da-al-zhin-thin-moasi*	period ice cat
permit	*gos-shi-e*	permit
personnel	*da-ne-lei*	member
photograph	*beh-chi-ma-had-nil*	photograph
pill box	*bi-so-dih-dot-sahi-bi-tsah*	sick pig box
pinned down	*bil-dah-has-tanh-ya*	pinned down
plane	*tsidi*	bird
plasma	*dil-di-ghili*	plasma
point	*be-so-de-dez-ahe*	pig point
pontoon	*tkosh-jah-da-na-elt*	floating barrel
postition	*bilh-has-ahn*	postition
possible	*ta-ha-ah-tay*	possible
post	*sah-dei*	post
prepare	*hash-tay-ho-dit-ne*	prepare
present	*cut*	now
previous	*bih-tse-dih*	previous
primary	*altseh-nan-day-hi-gih*	first position
priority	*hane-pesodi*	priority
probable	*da-tsi*	probable
problem	*na-nish-tsoh*	big job

proceed	*nay-nih-jih*	go
progress	*nah-sai*	progress
protection	*ah-chanh*	self defense
provide	*yis-nil*	furnish
purple	*dinl-chi*	purple
pyrotechnic	*coh-na-chanh*	fancy fire
question	*ah-jah*	ear
quick	*shil-loh*	quick
radar	*esat-tsanh*	listen
raid	*dez-jay*	raid
railhead	*a-de-geh-hi*	shipping & receiving point
railroad	*konh-na-al-bansi-bi-thin*	railroad
rallying	*a-lah-na-o-glalih*	gathering
range	*an-zah*	distance
rate	*gah-eh-yahn*	rabbit ate
ration	*na-a-jah*	ration
ravine	*chush-ka*	ravine
reach	*il-day*	arrived
ready	*kut*	ready
rear	*be-ka-denh*	behind
receipt	*shoz-teh*	receipt
recommend	*che-ho-tai-tahn*	recommend
reconnaissance	*ha-a-cidi*	inspector
reconnoiter	*ta-ha-ne-al-ya*	make sure
record	*gah-ah-nah-kloli*	r-e-rope
red	*li-chi*	red
reef	*tsa-zhin*	black rock
re-embark	*eh-na-coh*	go in
refire	*na-na-coh*	again fire
regulate	*na-yel-na*	regulate
reinforce	*nal-dzil*	reinforce
relief	*aganh-tol-jay*	relief
relieved	*nah-jih-co-nal-ya*	removed
reorganize	*ha-dit-zah*	reorganize
replacement	*ni-na-do-nil*	replacement
report	*who-neh*	got word
representatives	*tka-naz-nili*	triple men
request	*jo-kayed-goh*	ask for
reserve	*hesh-j-e*	reserve
restrict	*ba-ho-chini*	restricted
retire	*ah-hos-teend*	retire
retreat	*ji-din-nes-chane*	retreat
return	*na-dzah*	came back
reveal	*who-neh*	reveal
revert	*na-si-yiz*	turn around
revetment	*ba-nas-cla*	corner

ridge	*gah-ghil-keid*	rabbit ridge
riflemen	*be-al-do-hosteen*	riflemen
river	*toh-yil-kal*	much water
robot bomb	*a-ye-shi-na-tah-ih*	egg fly
rocket	*lesz-yil-beshi*	sand boil
roll	*yeh-mas*	roll
round	*naz-pas*	circle
route	*gah-bih-tkeen*	rabbit trail
runner	*nih-dzid-teih*	runner
sabotage	*a-tkel-yah*	hindered
saboteur	*a-tkel-el-ini*	trouble maker
sailors	*cha-le-gai*	white caps
salvage	*na-has-glah*	pick them up
sat	*bih-la-sana-cid-da-hi*	apple sitting
scarlet/red	*lhe-chi*	red
schedule	*beh-eh-ho-zini*	schedule
scout	*ha-a-sid-al-sizi-gih*	short reconnaissance
screen	*besh-na-nes-dizi*	screen
seamen	*tkal-kah-dineh-ih*	seamen
secret	*bah-has-tkih*	secret
sector	*yoehi*	sector
secure	*ye-dzhe-al-tsisi*	small security
seize	*yeel-stod*	seize
select	*be-tah-has-gla*	took out
semi colon	*da-ahl-zhin-bi-tsa-na-dahl*	dot drop
set	*dzeh-cid-da-hi*	elk sitting
shackle	*di-bah-nesh-gohz*	shackle
shell	*be-al-doh-be-ca*	shell
shore	*tah-bahn*	shore
short	*be-oh*	short
side	*bosh-keesh*	side
sight	*ye-el-tsanh*	seen
signal	*na-eh-eh-gish*	by signs
simplex	*alah-ih-ne-tih*	inner wire
sit	*tkin-cid-da-hi*	ice sitting
situate	*a-ho-tay*	situate
smoke	*lit*	smoke
sniper	*oh-behi*	pick 'em off
space	*be-tkah*	between
special	*e-yih-sih*	main thing
speed	*yo-zons*	swift motion
sporadic	*ah-na-ho-neil*	now and then
spotter	*eel-tsay-i*	spotter
spray	*klesh-so-dilzin*	snake pray
squadron	*nah-ghizi*	squash
storm	*ne-ol*	storm

straff	na-wo-ghi-goid	hoe
straggler	chy-ne-de-dahe	straggler
strategy	na-ha-tah	strategy
stream	toh-ni-lih	running water
strength	dzhel	strength
stretch	desz-tsood	stretch
strike	nay-dal-ghal	strike
strip	ha-tih-jah	strip
stubborn	nil-ta	stubborn
subject	na-nish-yazzie	small job
submerged	tkal-cla-yi-yah	went under water
submit	a-nih-leh	send
subordinate	al-khi-nal-dzl	helping each other
succeed	yah-tay-go-e-elah	make good
success	ut-zah	it is done
successful	ut-zah-ha-dez-bin	it is done well
successive	ut-zah-sid	success scar
such	yis-cleh	sox (socks)
suffer	to-ho-ne	suffer
summary	shin-go-bah	summer Mary
supplementary	tka-go-ne-nan-dey-he	third position
supply	nal-yeh-hi	supply
supply ship	nalga-hi-tsin-nah-ailh	supply ship
support	ba-ah-hot-gli	depend
surrender	ne-na-cha	surrender
surround	naz-pas	surround
survive	yis-da-ya	survive
system	di-ba-tsa-as-zhi-bi-tsin	system
tactical	e-chihn	tactical
take	gah-tahn	take
tank	chay-da-gahi	tortoise
tank destroyer	chay-da-gahi-nail-tsaidi	tortoise killer
target	wol-doni	target
task	tazi-na-eh-dil-kid	turkey ask
team	deh-na-as-tso-si	tea mouse
terrace	ali-khi-ho-ne-oha	terrace
terrain	tashi-na-hal-thin	turkey rain
territory	ka-yah	land
that	tazi-cha	turkey hat
the	cha-gee	blue jay
their	bih	their
thereafter	ta-zi-kwa-i-be-ka-di	turkey here after
these	cha-gi-o-eh	the see
they	ni-ghai	they
this	di	this
together	ta-bilh	with

torpedo	*lo-be-ca*	fish shell
total	*ta-al-so*	total
tracer	*beh-na-al-kah-hi*	tracer
traffic diagram	*hane-ba-na-as-dzoh*	diagram story line
train	*coh-nai-ali-bahn-si*	train
transportation	*a-hah-da-a-cha*	transportation
trench	*e-gade*	trench
triple	*tka-ih*	triple
troops	*nal-deh-hi*	troops
truck	*chido-tso*	big auto
type	*alth-ah-a-teh*	type
under	*bi-yah*	under
unidentified	*do-bay-hosen-e*	unknown
unit	*da-az-jah*	bunched
unshackle	*no-da-eh-nesh-gohz*	unshackle
until	*uh-quo-ho*	until
vicinity	*na-hos-ah-gih*	there about
village	*chah-ho-oh-lhan-ih*	many shelter
visibility	*nay-es-tee*	visibility
vital	*ta-eh-ye-sy*	vital
warning	*bilh-he-neh*	warning
was	*ne-teh*	was
water	*tkoh*	water
wave	*yilh-kolh*	wave
weapons	*beh-dah-a-hi-jih-gani*	fighting weapons
well	*to-ha-ha-dlay*	well
when	*gloe-eh-na-ah-wo-hai*	weasel hen
where	*gloe-ih-qui-ah*	weasel here
which	*gloe-ih-a-hsi-tlon*	weasel tied together
will	*gloe-ih-dot-sahi*	sick weasel
wire	*besh-tsosie*	thin wire
with	*bilh*	with
within	*bilh-bigih*	within
without	*ta-gaid*	without
wood	*chiz*	fire wood or wood
wounded	*cah-da-khi*	wounded
yard	*a-del-tahl*	step
zone	*bih-na-has-dzoh*	area

Appendix 2: Navajo Code Talkers: an honor roll

The following is a list compiled from records of known Navajo Code Talkers from the Navajo Nation Museum in Window Rock, Arizona; and the books "Navajo Weapon: The Navajo Code Talkers," by Sally McClain (Tucson: Rio Nuevo Press, 1981), and "Our Fathers, Our Grandfathers, Our Heroes …: The Navajo Code Talkers of World War II" (Gallup: Circle of light Navajo Educational Project, 2004). My deepest apologies for any omissions.

Akee, Dan
Alfred, Johnny (John Alfred)
Alfred, Perry
Anderson, Edward
Anthony, Franklin
Apache, Jimmie
Arviso, Bennie
Ashike, Earl
Ashley, Regis
Attikai, Harold
Augustine, John
Ayze, Lewis
Babiya, Don
Bahe, Henry
Bahe, Woody
Baldwin, Benjamin
Beard, Harold
Becenti, Ned
Becenti, Roy L.
Bedoni, Sidney
Begay, Carlos
Begay, Charlie H.
Begay, Charlie S.
Begay, Charlie Y.
Begay, Charlie Tsosie
Begay, Flemming D.
Begay, George K.
Begay, Henry
Begay, Jerry C.
Begay, Jimmie
Begay, Joe
Begay, Lee.
Begay, Leo
Begay, Leonard
Begay, Notah
Begay, Paul
Begay, Roy L.
Begay, Samuel H.

Begay, Thomas H.
Begay, Walter
Begay, Walter Kescoli
Begay, Willie K.
Begay, Wilson J.
Begody, David M.
Begody, Roger
Belinda, Wilmer
Belone, Harry
Benallie, Jimmie D.
Benally, Harrison Lee
Benally, Harry
Benally, Jimmie L.
Benally, John Ashi
Benally, Samuel
Bentone, Willie
Bernard, John
Betone, Lloyd
Bia, Andrew
Billey, Wilfred
Billie, Ben
Billiman, Howard
Billison, Dr. Samuel
Billy, Sam Jones
Bitsie, Peter J.
Bitsie, Wilsie
Bitsoi, Delford
Bizardie, Jesse
Black, Jesse
Blatchford, Paul
Bluehorse, David
Bowman, John Henry
Bowman, Robert
Brown, Arthur
Brown, Clarence Paul
Brown, Cosy
Brown, John, Jr.
Brown, Nelson A.

Brown, Tsosie Herman
Brown, William Tully
Buck, Wilford
Burke, Bobby
Burnie, Jose
Burnside, Francis A.
Burr, Sandy
Cadman, William
Calledito, Andrew
Carroll, Oscar Tsosie
Cattle Chaser, Dennis
Cayedito, Del
Cayedito, Ralph
Charley, Carson Bahe
Charlie, Sam
Chase, Frederick
Chavez, George
Chee, John
Clah, Stewart
Clark, Jimmie
Clauschee, Guy
Claw, Thomas
Cleveland, Benjamin
Cleveland, Billie
Cleveland, Ned
Cody, Leslie
Cohoe, James Charles
Craig, Bob Etsitty
Crawford, Eugene
Crawford, Karl Lee
Cronemeyer, Walter
Crosby, Billy
Csinnjinni, Carl
Curley, David
Curley, Rueban
Dale, Ray
Damon, Anson C.
Damon, Llowell Smith
Davis, Tully
Deal, Martin Dale
Dehiya, Dan
Dennison, George H.
Dennison, Leo
Dixon, James
Dodge, Jerome Cody
Dooley, Richard

Doolie, John
Draper, Nelson
Draper, Teddy, Sr.
Etsicitty, Kee
Etsitty, Deswood
Evans, Harold
Foghorn, Ray
Foster, Harold Y.
Fowler, King
Francisco, Jimmy
Freeman, Edwin
Gatewood, Joseph P.
George, William
Gishal, Milton Miller
Gleason, Jimmie
Goldtooth, Emmett
Goodluck, John
Goodman, Billie
Gorman, Dr. Carl N.
Gorman, Tom
Gray, Harvey
Grayson, Bill L.
Greymountain, Yazzie
Guerito, Billy Lewis
Gustine, Tully
Guy, Charles
Harding, Ben William
Harding, Jack W.
Hardy, Tom
Harrison, Emmett
Harrison, Tom
Haskie, Ross
Hawthorne, Roy Orville
Haycock, Bud
Hemstreet, Leslie
Henry, Albert
Henry, Edmund Juam
Henry, Kent Carl
Hickman, Dan Junian
Holiday, Calvin
Holiday, Samuel Tom
Housewood, Johnson
Housteen, Dennie
Howard, Ambrose
Hubbard, Arthur Jose
Hudson, Lewey

Hunter, Tom
Ilthma, Oscar B.
James, Benjamin
James, Billie
James, George B.
Jenson, Nevy
Johle, Elliott
John, Charlie T.
Johns, Edmund
Johns, Leroy M., Sr.
Johnny, Earl
Johnson, Deswood R.
Johnson, Frances T.
Johnson, Johnnie
Johnson, Peter
Johnson, Ralph
Jones, Jack
Jones, Tom H, Jr.
Jordan, David
Jose, Teddy
June, Allen Dale
June, Floyd
Keams, Percy
Keedah, Wilson
Kellwood, Joe H.
Kescoli, Alonzo
Ketchum, Bahe
Kien, William
King, Jimmy
Kinlacheeny, Paul
Kinsel, John
Kirk, George H.
Kirk, Leo
Kiyaani, Mike
Kontz, Rex T.
Lapahie, Harrison
Largo, James
Leonard, Alfred
Leroy, George
Leroy, John
Leuppe, Edward
Little, Keith M.
Lopez, Tommy K.
MacDonald, Peter
Malone, Max
Malone, Rex

Malone, Robert
Maloney, James
Maloney, Paul E.
Manuelito, Ben C.
Manuelito, Ira
Manuelito, James C.
Manuelito, Johnny R.
Manuelito, Peter
Marianito, Frank
Mark, Robert
Martin, Matthew
Martinez, Jose
McCabe, William
McCraith, Archibald
Mike, King Paul
Miles, General
Moffitt, Tom Clah
Morgan, Herbert
Morgan, Jack C.
Morgan, Ralph
Morgan, Sam
Morris, Joe
Moss, George Alfred
Multine, Oscar P.
Murphy, Calvin H.
Nagurski, Adolph N.
Nahkai, James T., Sr.
Nakaidinae, Peter, Sr.
Napa, Martin Felix
Na(e?)swood, Johnson
Negale, Harding
Newman, Alfred
Nez, Arthur
Nez, Chester
Nez, Freeland
Nez, Howard
Nez, Howard Hosteen
Nez, Isreal Hosteen
Nez, Jack
Nez, Sidney
Notah, Roy
Notah, Willie Anthony
O'Dell, Billy
Oliver, Lloyd
Oliver, Willard V.
Otero, Tom

Paddock, Layton
Pahe, Robert D.
Palmer, Joe
Parrish, Paul A.
Patrick, Amos Roy
Pattterson, David Earl
Peaches, Alfred James
Peshlakai, Sam
Pete, Frank Denny
Peterson, Joe, Sr.
Pinto, Guy
Pinto, Senator John
Platero, Richard
Preston, Jimmie
Price, Joe F.
Price, Wilson H.
Reed, Sam
Roanhorse, Harry C.
Sage, Andy
Sage, Denny
Salabiye, Jerry E.
Sandoval, Merril Leo
Sandoval, Peter P.
Sandoval, Samuel F.
Sandoval, Thomas
Scott, John
Sells, John C.
Shields, Freddie
Shorty, Dooley
Shorty, Robert T.
Silversmith, Joe A.
Silversmith, Sammy
Singer, Oscar Jones
Singer, Richard
Singer, Tom
Skeet, Wilson Chee
Slinkey, Richard T.
Slivers, Albert James
Slowtalker, Balmer
Smiley, Arcenio
Smith, Albert
Smith, Enoch
Smith, George
Smith, Raymond R.
Smith, Samuel Jesse
Soce, George B.

Sorrell, Benjamin G.
Sorrel, Jerome
Spencer, Harry
Tabaha, Johnnie
Tah, Alfred
Tah, Edward
Talley, John N.
Tallsalt, Bert
Thomas, Edward
Thomas, Richard
Thompson, Clare M.
Thompson, Everett M.
Thompson, Francis T.
Thompson, Frank T.
Thompson, Nelson S.
Todacheene, Carl Leonard
Todacheene, Frank Carl
Tohe, Benson
Toledo, Bill Henry
Toledo, Curtis
Toledo, Frank
Toledo, Preston
Toledo, Willie
Towne, Joseph H.
Towne, Zane
Tracey, Peter
Tso, Chester H.
Tso, Howard B.
Tso, Paul Edward
Tso, Samuel
Tsosie, Alfred
Tsosie, Cecil G.
Tsosie, Collins D.
Tsosie, David W.
Tsosie, Harry
Tsosie, Howard
Tsosie, Howard J.
Tsosie, Kenneth
Tsosie, Samuel, Sr.
Tsosie, Woody B.
Upshaw, John
Upshaw, William
Vandever, Joe
Visalia, Buster
Wagner, Oliver
Wallace, Stephan P.

Walley, Robert
Werito, John
Whitman, Joe Reid
Whitman, Lyman J.
Willetto, Frank
Willetto, Frank Chee
Williams, Alex
Williams, Kenneth
Willie, George B.
Willie, John
Wilson, William
Wilson, William Dean
Woody, Clarence Bahi
Yazhe, Earnest
Yazhe, Harrison A.
Yazza, Peter
Yazza, Vincent
Yazzie, Charlie H.
Yazzie, Clifton
Yazzie, Daniel
Yazzie, Eddie Melvin
Yazzie, Edison Kee
Yazzie, Felix
Yazzie, Francis
Yazzie, Frank H.
Yazzie, Harding
Yazzie, Harold
Yazzie, Joe Shorty
Yazzie, John
Yazzie, Justin D.
Yazzie, Reverend Lemuel
Yazzie, Ned
Yazzie, Pahe D.
Yazzie, Peter
Yazzie, Raphael D.
Yazzie, Robert
Yazzie, Sam
Yazzie, William
Yellowhair, Leon
Yellowhair, Stanley
Yellowman, Howard
Yoe, George
Zah, Henry

Index

Navajo Code Talker Carl Gorman on Saipan, June 27, 1944. His son, the late R. C. Gorman, was an illustrious Navajo artist. A superb artist himself, Carl Gorman designed the logo for the Navajo Code Talkers Association seen throughout this book. It is depicted in color on the back cover.
Photo courtesy National Archives.

On February 28, 2008, almost 63 years after the end of World War Two and nearly 40 years after the Navajo Code was finally declassified, the Navajo Code Talkers were honored in Phoenix. The occasion was the dedication of a 16 foot tall bronze statue designed by the Navajo-Ute artist Oreland C. Joe.

The statue is located in Wesley Bolin Memorial Plaza near Arizona's Capitol building.
Photos by Stephen Mack.

The dates and venues of interviews used in this book are as follows:

Keith Little
interview 1: Window Rock, Arizona, August 21, 2006
interview 2: Window Rock, Arizona, October 28, 2007
interview 3: Window Rock, Arizona, January 23, 2008

Samuel Tso
interview 1: Gallup, New Mexico, February 17, 2007
interview 2: Gallup, New Mexico, July 9, 2007

Kee Etsicitty
interview: Albuquerque, New Mexico, December 8-9, 2007

Jack Jones
interview: near Espanola, New Mexico, August 17, 2007

Alfred Newman
interview: Albuquerque, New Mexico, April 5, 2007

Chester Nez
interview 1: Albuquerque, New Mexico, March 6, 2007
interview 2: Albuquerque, New Mexico, December 7, 2007

Alfred Peaches
interview 1: Winslow, Arizona, August 28, 2007
interview 2: Winslow, Arizona, January 4, 2008

Bill Toledo
interview 1: Laguna, New Mexico, November 9, 2005
interview 2: Albuquerque, New Mexico, December 7, 2007

Stephen Mack, of Tohono O'odham descent, attended college at the University of Minnesota (Twin Cities campus), and graduated from the Institute of American Indian Arts in Santa Fe, New Mexico, and the University of New Mexico, Albuquerque. He has served as a volunteer for the Navajo Code Talkers Association for over three years.

His first book was the non-fiction "Walters' World: His Comic Postcards, His Art."

The Navajo Code Talkers Association is a nonprofit organization dedicated to the preservation of their legacy. For further information, the latest news, or to make a donation, please visit their website at navajocodetalkers.org .